I0168808

The 87-Fold Path
to Being the
Best Martial Artist

© 2014 by Kris Wilder and Lawrence A. Kane

All rights reserved. Reproduction of any part or the whole of this work in any form without prior written permission from the copyright owners is prohibited. No part of this publication may be reproduced, stored in or introduced into a retrieval system, or transmitted in any form or by any means (electronic, mechanical, photocopying, recording, or otherwise), without authorization. To request the authors' consent to reproduce any portions of this work please contact the authors through their website at

www.westseattlekarate.com.

Ordering Information:
Special offers and signed copies are available. For details, contact the publisher at the website above.

ISBN-13: 978-0692341834
ISBN-10: 0692341838

First Edition November, 2014

Stock photography and portraits, by Lawrence A. Kane
Cover and interior design by Kamila Z. Miller, www.wyrdgoat.com

Disclaimer

Information in this book is distributed "As Is," without warranty. Nothing in this document constitutes a legal opinion nor should any of its contents be treated as such. Neither the authors nor the publisher shall have any liability with respect to information contained herein. Further, neither the authors nor the publisher have any control over or assume any responsibility for websites or external resources referenced in this book.

The 87-Fold Path to Being the Best Martial Artist

87 Social and Psychological Tips for Living Beyond the Physical

Kris Wilder
Lawrence A. Kane

Stickman Publications

Burien, Washington

CONTENTS

INTRODUCTION...i

HOLDING BACK INSTRUCTION...1

PRECISELY WHEN I WANT IT..5

MARTIAL ARTS INFORMATION..9

THE RED PEN..13

CALCULATORS, LAB COATS, AND THE WEB.............................17

THE MOMENT AN INSTITUTION...21

HOLLYWOOD CHANGED YOU, MAN..25

FIRE YOUR STUDENTS..29

THE DRUNKEN MONKEY..33

LEAVING THE DOJO..37

A PROPHET IN YOUR OWN LAND...41

I THOUGHT I WOULD HAVE A DOJO FULL OF FIRE-EATERS....45

MY FRIEND AND HIS PHONE NUMBER....................................49

I GOT A GOOD FIGHT FOR YOU...53

SMITH'S RULES OF DESIGN #6..57

THREE PRINCIPLES...61

KARATE & THE BEATLES...65

PEOPLE TIRE OF TRUTH...67

BOUNDARIES...71

THINGS GET VERY STILL..75

THE DUNNING-KRUGER EFFECT...79

THE OLD MAN MEDICI...83

BAD AUTHORITY...87

CHALLENGING PLAYGROUNDS..89

15 MINUTES AND 30 YEARS..93

BE AWARE... PFFFT... USELESS..97

LAWS OF NATURE & THE CROSSWALK...101

FOOD ALLERGIES MAKE KIDS A TARGET OF BULLIES........................105

SIMPLICITY...109

YOUR OWN SENSE OF SUCCESS..113

PURE BREEDS AND MUTTS...117

TELL BRUCE LEE IT HAPPENED...119

PERFECT LIGHT AND MAKEUP..123

TELL BRUCE LEE, ALL IS NOT LOST...127

STREET KIDS AND THE DOJO..131

MARTIAL ARTS TRAINING TIP #62...135

NOTHING SAYS LOSER LIKE...139

THAT'S PROFILING DAD..143

HELPING KARATEKA ACHIEVE THEIR GOALS..................................147

SOCRATES, RORY MILLER, AND EARTHWORMS...............................151

SMITH'S RULES OF DESIGN, #3...155

DIRT UNDER YOUR FINGERNAILS..159

THE CONCLUSION COMES WITH CLARITY.......................................161

NOT ME, NOT HERE!...165

KARATE PURITANS...169

SMITH'S RULES OF DESIGN, #7...173

I QUIT DRINKING MY COFFEE...177

THE INTERNETS...181

TEENAGE GIRL GETS A BEAT-DOWN..185

ONE WHO REFLECTS UPON..191

POETRY AND TEACHING...195

THEY HID IT, BUT NOT IN THE FORM..199

OBSESSION IN THE PURSUIT..203

SMITH'S RULES OF DESIGN, #2...207

I HIRED A JUDOKA...211

ENTER THE DRAGON..215

AWARENESS...221

TRADITION AND BUNNY HOPS..225

BLACK EYES AND MAT-RASH...229

TO BE A BLACK BELT..233

DECISION MAKING...235

SOUND LIKE A WUSS..239

MAKING PROMISES... AND KEEPING THEM......................................241

BANKRUPTCY OF PURSE OR BANKRUPTCY OF LIFE.......................245

CULTURAL REASSURANCE..249

ONE BAD APPLE DON'T SPOIL THE WHOLE BUNCH, GIRL............253

I WAS CHANGED BY THE MARTIAL ARTS..257

BROAD OR DEEP...261

SPREAD IT AROUND...265

TIME AND TIME MANAGEMENT..269

SOCIETY OF SQUEALERS..273

HARD EARNED WISDOM..277

PERSONAL PRACTICE..281

KILL THE MESSENGER... AND ESPECIALLY THE MESSAGE.............285

AN ODD COMBINATION OF EMOTIONS...289

MADONNA VS. DESCARTES..293

WELCOME THE AMAZING RANDI...297

I DO MY KARATE THE OLD FASHIONED WAY....................................301

THE GOOD PEOPLE..305

MAGIC AND KARATE...309

MIND YOUR OWN BUSINESS, PUNK!...313

IF YOU JUST SWALLOW EVERYTHING...317

YOGA-IN-A-BOX..321

SEE, DO, TEACH..323

THE OLD GUYS..327

SMITH'S RULES OF DESIGN, #4...331

CHICKEN WIRE, BLACK PAINT AND NEON, OH, MY!.......................335

CONCLUSION..339

ABOUT THE AUTHORS...341

OTHER WORKS BY THE AUTHORS...345

INTRODUCTION

"Your hand opens and closes, opens and closes. If it were always a fist or always stretched open, you would be paralyzed. Your deepest presence is in every small contracting and expanding, the two as beautifully balanced and coordinated as birds' wings."

– Rumi

People who don't understand violence don't understand the martial arts. They claim that the arts propagate violence, but the truth is that the more you know about physical conflict, the less likely you are to engage in violence.

In fact, violence is a very small part of martial arts.

Let's do the math. In one year there are 31,536,000 seconds. Multiply that by 25 years for the age of a young man who studies martial arts and the result is 788,400,000 seconds. The average street fight lasts about 10 seconds, give or take a few. Now let's pick out of the sky the numeral three, and call that the number of fights the average 25-year-old civilian has been involved in. Perhaps that's high, maybe it's low, but it helps to make our point... In 25 years this average male martial artist has fought for a grand total of half a minute! And yet when we are on the training floor, we spend almost all of our time preparing for those 30 seconds.

If you do not find something larger than base violence attached your efforts, your martial arts adventure will come to an end. You will quit.

The reason for leaving is that you will find the repetitiveness of the training boring—you're working the same stuff over and over again, honing it, but never using it. Further you will innately discover that you live in imbalance. Practice that is balanced survives, just like the person who eats a well-balanced diet, or holds work and play in proper proportion, seeking each element of life in the correct time and in the right amounts. Practice that's imbalanced... ultimately it's a temporary condition.

We like the following quote from Dean Koontz, American suspense novelist, who in *Dead and Alive* wrote, "Maybe if everything was beautiful, nothing would be. People saw one thing, they swooned over it. They saw this other thing, they pounded it with sticks. Maybe there had to be variety for life to work. Swoon over everything, you get bored. Beat everything with a stick—boring."

For our purposes we will taking out the word "stick" and replace it with "fist." Now his quote reads: "Maybe if everything was beautiful, nothing would be. People saw one thing, they swooned over it. They saw this other thing, they pounded it with fists. Maybe there had to be variety for life to work. Swoon over everything, you get bored. Beat everything with a fist—boring."

At a 2005 Stanford University commencement address, Steve Jobs said, "You can't connect the dots looking forward you can only connect them looking backwards. So you have to trust that the dots will somehow connect in your future. You have to trust in something: Your gut, destiny, life, karma, whatever... Because believing that the dots will connect down the road will give you the confidence to follow your heart, even when it leads you off the well-worn path." In this book we present to you a path, one designed to open the door to a more balanced perspective of the martial arts.

The 87-Fold Path is our way of giving you some ideas to ponder that are uniquely tailored for the martial artist. For those that resonate, we include instructions for making them real, suggested ways in which you might apply the concepts, integrate them into your world of thought—or possibly reject them altogether.

It's all up to you.

CHAPTER ONE

HOLDING BACK INSTRUCTION

"A lie that is half-truth is the darkest of all lies."

– Alfred Tennyson

We're rabid (American) football fans who regularly watch professional, college, and even high school games. Our sons who play together on a high school varsity team have aspirations to make it into the college ranks, so we've been talking to a lot coaches recently. Like any profession, college football coaches have a diverse range of personalities and perspectives, but one thing we hear is consistent across the entire group. These coaches all know that they will have limited time with each player on their team, five years maximum (assuming a redshirt season) apiece. After that the players are gone. No comebacks. NCAA rules mandate that once a player has used up his (or her) eligibility he will never play another down of college football again. Ever!

This inevitable termination shapes the coaches' perspectives. These coaches want to win—their careers, livelihoods, and reputations are dependent upon victories—and to do that their players must become the best that they can be in the shortest amount of time possible. That starts with recruiting the finest talent they can acquire, of course, but the players must sustain an extremely high level of play too, starting strong and steadily improving from the moment they enroll in school through graduation.

What environments does this dynamic create? One of giving, giving everything you have as a coach, finding the best way to reach each young man, assure he will understand, and guarantee to the extent possible that he will respond. These coaches give everything they have to make their players better, safer, stronger, and smarter. The last thing you will ever hear an elite coach say is, "I am holding back teaching from you. You're not ready." Instead, they say things like, "You are going rise to the challenge because you have it in you."

Sadly, it is not uncommon to hear martial arts instructors say, "You're not ready. I'm not going to show you that yet." We rarely hear them say, "I am going to teach and I know you will rise to the challenge." How egocentric is that? How dysfunctional? If football coaches are teaching to develop skill and prevent injury, what is the martial arts instructor who claims to be holding back instruction doing?

Making it real...

One of the healthier martial traditions is bowing to (or saluting in some way) one's training partners before and after practicing together. It's not only a sign of respect, but also recognition that there is something to be learned from everyone who is willing to share, no matter what their rank might be. Challenge yourself next time you step into the *dojo* (training hall). Have you been holding back? Make a concerted effort to share one thing—one trick, tip, or tactic from your "A-list"—with each person you work with every single time you train. In helping others improve you better yourself too.

CHAPTER TWO

PRECISELY WHEN I WANT IT

"Be a yardstick of quality. Some people aren't used to an environment where excellence is expected."

– Steve Jobs

Standing in line at a fast food restaurant the person in front of me requested, "Extra, extra, extra crispy French fries." Seriously?! At a fast food restaurant? Yup, that's exactly what the guy ordered. And, sadly, it wasn't the first time I'd heard a person request something like that.

Simply ordering a fresh cup of coffee can be challenging because of the vast variety of options you can choose, or demand, even at convenience stores. Everything is a double half-caf, half-mocha, espresso macchiato explosion with shaved chocolate sprinkles or some such nonsense.

Health clubs are open twenty-four hours. Order just about anything you want online and it can be delivered to your door the next day. Welcome to the fast food generation. Heck, there's even an ad campaign touting the slogan, "I want it now!"

Most things today seem to be about convenience, speed and consumption, all the while meeting the consumer's tailored, exacting requests. Customer-centric, sure. But it goes overboard. How often do we hear people get bent out of shape for the smallest thing: "This is *not* what I ordered!" "You couldn't match the color exactly?" "Those times are not good for me." "How can you treat me like that?!" People seem to take an awful lot of pride in victimhood nowadays.

A good martial arts studio, on the other hand, is a throwback to another time, a time where this egocentric behavior had no place. Here are three tips to make sure you, with little effort, can become that extra, extra, extra crispy, hopelessly entitled, effete martial artist:

- ◆ Find an average leader: Somebody who will let you do all the things you want to do because... well, you want to do them. Curriculum? That's not for you, right?

- ◆ Pay attention to the details: To the point of excluding the big picture entirely; or, instead, just make up your own, private big picture and then you can just focus on what supports your desires to the exclusion of all else. Mmmm... extra, extra, extra, crispy fries. With pink Himalayan salt!

- ◆ Reach real far, real fast: Take those shortcuts to mastery that you know are there and if your instructor won't show you them, then refer back to the first tip.

Cynicism aside, martial arts are a rare pursuit, anachronistic yet fully functional in a modern world. And they take time, discipline, and patience to master. Instructors, good ones anyway, don't hold back. But, they don't shortcut the process either. Holistic, realistic, and practical, these are the hallmarks of exemplary instruction.

Making it real...

Are you entitled? Really, are you? Does pride, intolerance, or impetuosity get in the way of your training? *Sensei* in Japanese translates as "instructor," but it also means "one who has gone before." He or she has been there, done that, and learned a thing or two along the way. Make the most of your instructor's wisdom by understanding his/her program and (unless it is irremediably flawed) embracing it wholeheartedly. We're not suggesting blind obedience here, but if you're paying an expert to teach you something, let him apply his/her expertise. *Sensei* likely knows best.

CHAPTER THREE

MARTIAL ARTS INFORMATION

"'Well,' said Pooh, 'What I like best,' and then he had to stop and think. Because although eating honey was a very good thing to do, there was a moment just before you began to eat it which was better than when you were, but he didn't know what it was called."

– A. A. Milne

When we started training back in the 70s, martial arts information and instruction were at a premium. No videos to speak of existed (just some Super 8 and 35mm film that few could obtain), no web, and no YouTube. Only a couple of magazines were on the market and what books you even knew about took six to eight weeks for mail-order delivery. That meant you valued every piece of instruction you could get your hands on—scraping together enough money to order a book that may not have anything at all to do with your art, just to get a little something extra besides what you learned once or twice a week on the training floor.

This brought a laser-like focus to your training. You worked what you had and you worked it hard. You tried to see what you could observe from as many angles as your mind would allow.

Today we have so much information at our fingertips it boggles the mind. For example, the web brings us YouTube videos galore; the struggle isn't finding what you want but rather vetting the quality of the thousands of examples you do find in order to identify the handful that are actually worth watching. Print and e-books abound, new magazines come and go, and message boards/online forums sprout like mushrooms (and are often fertilized in much the same way). And, seminars round out the monstrous amount of information that we can readily access.

This dynamic brings a dispersed view to your training. It makes students look frantically down every new avenue for that one "magic bullet" that is going to give them the edge. The fact of the matter is that too little information and too much information both mean hard training, but for very different reasons. With too little you can get stuck, whereas with too much you don't know where or how to focus.

Don't look too far ahead. Stay focused on what you are tasked with and polish that instead of simply seeking out the next big thrill. Concepts go broad and deep; there's far more to mastery than most folks realize when they begin the journey. In fact, in most arts the four to eight years spent earning a black belt (or sash) simply mean that you understand the fundamentals well enough that you are capable of deeper learning. The black belt is not a destination, but rather where the real journey begins.

Making it real...

Here is a simple test to tell if you are looking too far ahead. If you say to yourself "I can't wait to learn the next form, I've already done this one before," then you are in all likelihood looking too far ahead. If you are working old material with a new perspective, then that's about right. Like aging a fine wine, progress, real progress in the martial arts, can't be rushed.

CHAPTER FOUR

THE RED PEN

"Correction does much, but encouragement does more."

– Johann Wolfgang von Goethe

When Kris worked in Public Relations he met a guy named Carl who owned a very successful PR company. Carl was pleasant, calm, and generally a nice person. Smart too. He taught Kris something that we want to share: As Kris watched him proofread a press release prior to it going out to the media Carl rocked back in his chair and read the write-up in its entirety. He then leaned forward, handed it to the intern who had written it, and said, "Looks fine to me. Send it."

Press releases are a really big deal and getting them exactly right is important. After the intern left the room, Kris said, "Wow, she must be pretty good! No changes."

"Oh, I could have changed a few things, but they were personal preferences, not really structural," Carl replied. "I never read anybody's work with a pen in my hand."

"What do you mean by that?"

"Have you ever noticed that when people are handed a document, the first thing they do is pull out a pen and click that pen ready to mark the piece of paper up?"

"Yeah, I have."

"Well, I don't do it that way. I want to read the document first, take it all in, and see what they are trying to communicate instead of playing 'gotcha.'"

That conversation took place some twenty years ago, but it applies even more today than it did back then. Go read the comments on YouTube videos, blogs, or online movie reviews. It's rare that somebody simply posts something nice and moves on with their day. They all want to whip out their proverbial red pen and play the game of gotcha. More often than not comments start out pleasant enough yet also include, "but," "however," "that being said," or some other permutation of a conjunction that negates the former positive statement. Unfortunately this condition often spills over into martial arts schools too.

"That was a great *kata* (form) you just did, but..."

Look, most adults and a fair number of kids practice martial arts because they love them. Don't get out your pen, click it, and begin to mark it up student performances too soon. Let them make their own choices, put their own stamp on the art. See what they are about, where they are going, and then maybe weigh in with meaningful corrections.

Making it real...

That intern from twenty years ago, it's a safe bet that she felt very good about the press release, which means confidence. And, that breeds success. When we, as instructors, reach for the proverbial red pen too quickly, are we breeding success? Likely not. If you do need to make adjustments, strive to never correct more than three things during any one training session. Not only does that dampen enthusiasm, it tends to overwhelm too. We cannot and should not expect miracles, yet many instructors communicate in ways that make them appear to demand instantaneous perfection from their disciples as if they do. Clear, constructive feedback metered in small doses sets guiderails that help students succeed.

CHAPTER FIVE

CALCULATORS, LAB COATS, AND THE WEB

"With power comes the abuse of power. And where there are bosses, there are crazy bosses. It's nothing new."

– Judd Rose

A college professor showed a neat trick to use in meetings. He said, "When you need to get your point across, reach for a calculator. Everybody will defer to you." He was right; we have both used that trick or some variation of it several times since then. It's a ploy, one that implies expert knowledge that you may or may not actually possess. And it works.

Today, anyone can build or fake expertise. Technology allows for enormous amounts of information to be distributed quickly, efficiently, and ubiquitously—

self-published books, print-on-demand, Google, YouTube, and so on... It's easier now than at any time in history to find data, but in some ways harder than ever to find information.

As martial artists, we need to be very discerning, careful about our sources. Think of it this way: If a doctor in a lab coat says, "You have high blood pressure and you need medication or you risk a heart attack," is your answer, "Where do I get the prescription?" Or is it, "Huh, I wonder what my blood pressure is when I am not in the doctor's office?"

Would you get a second opinion if the diagnosis was cancer? Yes, yes you would. Why? Because your doctor would suggest it as a matter of course, even going so far as to provide you with a referral to make getting a second opinion easier to obtain. Why does he/she do that? Because doctors are wise enough to admit that they don't know everything. When a patient's life is on the line they take extra precautions to assure that the optimal treatment is administered, that everything is done right. Oftentimes that means helping patients become better educated on their condition so that they can make informed choices on how to proceed.

The challenge is that people are conditioned to trust authority—hierarchical authority, expert authority—folks they believe have power or knowledge that they themselves do not possess. Do you automatically defer to machines, lab coats, or martial arts instructors? Electronics fail, doctors get things wrong, and martial arts instructors... well, let's face it we can't all walk on water or part the Red Sea. We're not suggesting becoming a jerk and challenging everybody, but it is prudent to subtly question the who, what, when, where, and why of things.

You're a martial artist, right? Martial arts by definition are warlike and dangerous. If, for instance, all you're studying is techniques, that's much like learning how to drive a car without ever hearing the rules of the road. That's clearly problematic. Similarly, fights, even unavoidable ones, have aftermaths. We all know that when law enforcement officers, lawyers, doctors, or morticians get involved things tend not to end well those who participated in making bad things happen, but how many teachers gloss over those vital aspects of the arts in their instruction?

Be responsible to yourself and for yourself, especially when it comes to martial arts. Just because it comes from a calculator, or is wrapped in a lab coat or *dogi*, doesn't necessarily make it true.

Making it real...

Healthy skepticism can be a good thing. Learn how to scrutinize the information you receive by giving yourself a little homework: Regularly research one new fact about your art, something you can confirm from three independent sources (that don't cross-reference each other). Or, grab your local statutes and read up on self defense, then schedule a half hour (typically free) consultation with a good attorney and find out how relevant case laws have been interpreted. Or, attend a seminar with an instructor who practices a different style in order to broaden your perspective... You get the idea. Pick one new area to investigate each month, validating, invalidating, or expanding upon what your instructor(s) have told you, and keep at it each and every month for at least a year.

CHAPTER SIX

THE MOMENT AN INSTITUTION...

"The moment an institution, a belief system, or a person takes from me ownership of my pain, my suffering, my disease, my aging, or my death, it expropriates from me the ability to grow, develop, or have health in my own life."

– Ivan Illich

Every day we live in systems. As upstanding citizens we go along and get along. We rise when the electric alarm goes off telling us it is time to get up. We obey the laws, most of 'em anyway. We speak (or keep silent) the way our employers require.

We rarely question authority. When institutions demand our personal and private information, chances are good that we give it without hesitation. Heck, we're so used to paying taxes that are skimmed off the top of our paychecks, that we don't even know how much we're shelling out. Or, what it's being used for.

And, we do what our martial arts instructor(s) asks us to do as well. Oftentimes without thinking...

We get so accustomed to just giving ourselves away piece by piece, that as martial artists we need to raise a question about our approach from time to time in order to keep us grounded. Are we doing what is asked of us in our martial arts school because we have mindlessly complied, or are we doing it because we see benefit in the actions? Have we, without forethought, given ourselves over to our instructor?

What if you changed Ivan Illich's words above to reflect our martial art?

"The moment a *dojo*, a martial arts system, or a instructor takes from me ownership of my training, my growth, my technique, my freedom of action, or my identity outside of the *dojo*, it (or they) expropriates from me the ability to grow, develop, or have health in my own life."

Our culture today throughout much of the world is one of loss of personal power. Are you taking your precious personal time and giving that away too? We are not asking you to be the next revolutionary leader. We are, however, asking you to look at what you do and why you do it (or don't do it for that matter). Take control of your training. Make it yours.

Making it real...

Jot it down. Why are you training? What are your goals? Have they changed or evolved? While younger students are often drawn toward competition or camaraderie in the *dojo*, as they age and mature the focus often changes toward gaining a deeper understanding of the art, learning self-protection, seeking opportunities to teach, or even seeking spiritual enlightenment. Put your plan on paper, keep it current, and refer back to it from time to time to make sure you're still on track. If you're not furthering your goals, you're wasting your time.

CHAPTER SEVEN

HOLLYWOOD
CHANGED YOU, MAN

"Money and success don't change people; they merely amplify what is already there."

– Will Smith

You know the story: Money, titles, promotions, fame... it changes the person. You see it in real life and portrayed both on film and the small screen. The story of the lost way is so ubiquitous that it is found in myth and sacred documents alike from virtually every culture on the planet. You know the telltale comments people often say that indicate those who have lost their way: "Power changed them," "Success has spoiled them," or "I don't know them anymore." We're martial artists and authors, but we've had other careers too, spending time around politicians, law enforcement professionals, business leaders, soldiers, and educators, many whom have held or currently hold positions at the highest levels in their respective fields. And, we've seen "before" and "after," witnessed the changes too.

For example, Lawrence was on the interview committee for a new hire who over the course of 25 years went on to become senior vice president of a Fortune® 30 corporation. His dad was the lead over two different CEOs when they first started working at that same company as junior engineers. Two of the three changed significantly over time, eventually being fired for ethical lapses, whereas the third remained much the same and is still gainfully employed.

Based on these experiences and others, neither of us really believes that power changes people. Instead, we have found that power allows people to act the way they want to act. What we ultimately see is people behaving in ways that are consistent with their true nature, unrestricted by the gravity of rules that once governed their universe.

True leaders take on acquired positions of power with humility, respect, and an eye toward responsibility. They know themselves and stay true to their nature. And, they know that (to paraphrase the famous saying from spider-dude) greater power necessitates greater responsibility... and provides more opportunities for failure. It's easy for small-minded individuals to get so wrapped up in achieving some hard-sought result that they rationalize unscrupulous methods of getting there. Nevertheless, these true leaders' outer trappings may change, but internally they are the same person they were before their promotion to department head, master sergeant, CEO... or black belt.

Making it real...

Every heard of a personal mission statement? It's a Steven Covey thing, something you can read about in detail in his book *The 7 Habits of Highly Effective People*. If you find yourself drifting, out of sorts, or disgruntled it is oftentimes a result of straying from the essence of who you are or what you want to be at your core. Putting your values in writing and referring back to them from time to time helps you stay centered. Think about what's important. Write it down. You'll be far better for the experience.

CHAPTER EIGHT

FIRE YOUR STUDENTS

"If you can't describe what you are doing as a process, you don't know what you're doing."

– W. Edwards Deming

How many of us have seen the *dojo* bully? You know, that guy (or gal) who pushes training partners a little too much, strikes a little too hard, punishes when no one's looking, and relishes dishing out pain. You've seen him, worked with him, maybe even been picked on by him right? Is the bully one of your students? What about the time-sucker, the chronic-interrupter, or the imperious know-it-all? If so, why? Why on earth would you put up with that, sanction such dysfunctional behaviors in your school?

Sadly we have made that mistake too, let our good nature overrule common sense. We have extended the courtesy that, "With a little more work this student is going to come around," but predictably (in retrospect anyway) that was not at all what happened. What did occur was we gave an inch (of courtesy) and the student took the proverbial mile. And, we waited far too long to take action to rectify the situation.

Learn from our mistake. Fire your students! Yes, fire them, send them packing. We know that sounds harsh but if you discover that you have the wrong people in your class ask them to leave. If you are a business owner you have the right to refuse service carte blanche, no questions asked. If you work with a health club or such it is a little tricky as they will complain about you, but have the courage to make a decision and stick to your guns.

Now we're not suggesting being a jerk about it. Don't make scene, just pull the person aside and firmly but politely let them go. It can be outside on the sidewalk, after hours in the *dojo* when other students have left, or wherever you feel's appropriate. Here is the formula.

- Be swift.
- Use few words.
- Explain why the person is being asked to leave.
- Shut up; don't argue about it.

Here is an example.

"I have spoken to you several times about injuring other students. I have worked with you on your control and have given you time to correct your behavior, but that has not happened. I cannot

place other students at risk. Here is a refund for
the remainder of your dojo dues for this month.
You cannot train here anymore. I wish you well."

Correcting a mistake is usually painful and difficult
but it has to be done. In this example the instructor
made a series of bad decisions. He started training
somebody that he should not have, and then let
him (or her) hang around too long hoping for a
course correction that would never come. Sadly, if
you've been teaching long enough this sounds eerily
familiar, right?

A real life example from when Kris was a green belt:

After several warnings, the head instructor took
the offending student to the back of the *dojo* and
said, "You're strong when you face lower ranks.
I am tired of you injuring my students... Defend
yourself!" And then pow, pow, pow... it was fast,
it was merciless, and when it was done Kris's
sensei reached down, took the brown belt off the
student and said, "This is mine. Now, get out of
my *dojo!*"

Ah, the old days.

Making it real...

Never forget that as a martial arts instructor you're
teaching dangerous, possibly deadly stuff. If students
misuse what they've been taught it's on you. Perhaps
not legally in all instances, but certainly morally and
ethically. Even if you're not on the hook, whatever
happens you still need to be able to look at yourself

in the mirror each morning. That's a whole lot easier when you know you've done the right thing. This adage can help: If students don't understand the rules it's your fault. If they don't follow them, it's theirs'. Do what needs to be done; let the unworthy go.

CHAPTER NINE

THE DRUNKEN MONKEY

"I might be off on a rant here..."

– Dennis Miller

And now for an invective, didactic diatribe from Kris Wilder:

I might be off on a rant here... No "might" about it. I am off on a rant. However, I must rant, so hang on...

I have had many conversations with others about something called "The Drunken Monkey." The Drunken Monkey sits in the middle of your mind, wearing a fez, clanging the cymbals, and telling you in no uncertain terms that you are far less than you really are. But you know what is really more important than the false information he spews into your head? It is the fact that he makes that horrible racket, doesn't let you have any silence, any chance to think.

You know what power comes in silence... inspiration!

Edison used silence to help him create. He would sit quietly in a chair becoming still and silent, then the inspiration would come. His contemporary and rival Nikola Tesla lived a Spartan existence where he would often feed the pigeons from a park bench... in silence.

Today The Drunken Monkey has moved outside of our heads and lives in our televisions, the web, and our iPhones. These mechanisms have become tyrants of the mind... not just a funny-looking monkey spewing gibberish, but a malevolent tyrant. A tyrant who demands that whatever you are doing is not as important as what might be available on my smart phone, Facebook, Snapchat, or Twitter.

Not only is most social media a faux relationship with others, but celebrities and politicians have other people tweeting for them, making their feeds not only meaningless, "I'm getting a fruit smoothie!," but fake. More often than not these posts are not even genuine.

Now if you think that I am on my high horse, all holy and such, I have to admit that I can literally reach six inches from my desk and touch this week's *Entertainment Weekly* magazine. Yeah, I'm guilty of being "Old School," you know, print, with my meaningless content. However, I will give *Entertainment Weekly* credit in that it doesn't beep, ping, or ring at me demanding that I read with all immediacy about what Kevin Federline is eating or Kim Kardashian is wearing.

And now, for a moment of silence... You know, kinda like Edison and Tesla.

Thus endeth the rant.

Making it real...

We only have one life to live. Consequently our time is limited... and precious. Think about how much of it you devote to social media. Are Facebook, Twitter, LinkedIn, YouTube, Snapchat, and the like convenient ways of keeping in touch with friends or colleagues, or have they become a vacuous time-suck that wastes your day and drains your creative energies? Test yourself: Can you take a week off, devote a full seven days to other pursuits while not touching any form of social media? Go on, give it a shot. We dare you to try!

CHAPTER TEN

LEAVING THE DOJO

*"You remember only what you want to remember. You
know only what your heart allows you to know."*

– Amy Tan

A few years ago the building that the West Seattle
Karate Academy had been housed in for nearly a
decade was put up for sale. That meant that the *dojo*
had to move—a whole three long blocks down the
street mind you, but move it did.

The new space was a little bigger, a little nicer, and
right next to our chiropractor. Not bad. But, the old
place had character. History. There's something
about the sweat, the camaraderie, the focused
discipline that makes a training hall more than just
a building. Thinking back on the last few days in the

place becomes a moment turned into a sentimental accounting...

Looking over to the right was the window that Ito threw Devin into. That spot there is where Devin used duct tape and paper towels to stop the bleeding from the glass because we had run out of bandages. "Oh yeah," There's the other window, the one that Lawrence broke. There is the cabinet that Kris kicked; dent's still there... "Hmm, never did replace that broken door." "Ah, the wall that Ito threw Tony into, man, that left a big hole."

New mud, tape, and paint on the back wall, resurfaced to a smooth finish but not totally... a few bumps remain. "Oh yeah that's where Kris punched through the wall." "Huh, another bump; don't remember that one... big, too." "Lawrence broke that light; who was it that he threw into it again... can't remember." "When he inadvertently took that other light out with a *bo* (staff), the expression on his face was priceless—seemed like it took forever to clear all the glass shards off the floor."

Sniff the air. You can smell the late-night cooking from the catering company next door. When we first moved in, the space that catering company occupies was rented by a tattoo parlor, one that sold illegal weed out of the back. Despite the heat we had to close our back door most summer nights to keep the *ganja* smoke from wafting into the *dojo*.

The area above the door was where we stored the mats. Yeah, those mats covered up the .22 caliber bullet hole in the window. It is funny how Japanese and Okinawan visitors who are not allowed to own any type of firearms thought that tiny bullet hole was the most interesting thing they'd ever seen.

The wood floor we laid down held up well, despite years of use and abuse. We built a grid of 2x4s and plywood for strength and flexibility, then sealed and polished it with an industrial boat finish. Almost fondly we remember cleaning up the occasional blood and puke, getting down on the floor with water and bleach and scrub up accidents. Remember that kid who peed on the floor during class... sigh.

Reading back on what was written here it may have sounded like the old *dojo* was a horrible place, populated by irresponsible, macho jerks. But no, no it was not. If that were true then the *dojo* would be closed permanently because nobody would train at the West Seattle Karate Academy. These stories are just a result of focused training and the, oh, let's call it the "uneven character" of the neighborhood.

Well, the new *dojo* is great, a great facility and a place for focused training. It's a story waiting to be written. Nevertheless, locking the door one last time we can look back on the old place and smile...

Making it real...

Think about where you train. Is it a stand-alone *dojo*, a gymnasium, the basement of a YMCA? You may or may not get to choose the building or the layout, but you absolutely can determine your part in writing the story of the place. It's history. Think about what you want folks to remember from your contribution years from now when you are long gone. What would you like written? Think, then act.

CHAPTER ELEVEN

A PROPHET IN
YOUR OWN LAND

"It's easy to cry when you realize that everyone you love will reject you or die."

– Chuck Palahniuk

There is an old saying that a person cannot be a prophet in his or her own land. It's not just an adage, it is actually quite true. This speaks to a very pervasive attitude that most of us, probably all of us, have succumbed to at one time or another. Heck, even the bible says, "A prophet is not without honor, save in his own country, and in his own house."

A personal example that comes to mind concerns a guy on our local sports-radio scene who goes by the moniker "Softy." We both listen to sports radio regularly, and can remember when Softy was just an intern, the guy who did all the odd jobs, bad slots, and fill-in work that his station needed and no one else wanted to perform. Today he has a prime morning spot, one that Lawrence listens to on his morning drive to work most days.

Kris was in the *dojo* cleaning up and listening to Softy on the radio one day. At one point in the broadcast, he found himself disagreeing with what the show's host had to say regarding one of the local sports teams. He said to himself, "I knew you when you were an intern, you don't know what you are talking about!"

Clearly, that was just wrong on his part. He was mentally trying to force Softy back into a slot in time that he had long outgrown. Why? Because, if he was once "just" the intern, his position could not be credible. Illogical, clearly, but Kris put him down, if only in his own head, to make Softy fit into his line of thinking.

Oftentimes, we see other martial artists in this same light. We say things like, "I remember training with him way back when he was 10 years old." That's true, certainly, but students grow older, become wiser, get better, and in all likelihood are still in their prime, whereas we may have gotten older and better, but we might just have edged past your prime ourselves. There's much to learn from each newer generation.

What we're really getting at here is that instead of living in the past and judging people on what they were doing or were capable of when we first met them, it is important to accept them for who they are today. Whether it is in the role of a young college student, a first-time parent, or somebody who's left the nest and started his or her own martial arts school, everyone is the sum of their experiences. We all learn, grow, and improve over time. Sure, everyone knows that intellectually, but at the gut level it's something we often forget.

By taking people at current value as well as in the context of how far they've come we get a far better picture of their worth. We may also find that this time around they may have something to share.

Making it real...

This applies a bit more to long-time martial artists than it does to folks who have recently begun their training, but familiarity breeds... well, under-appreciation. To make the most out of your training, find one new thing, no matter how small, that you can learn from everyone you interact with in the *dojo* each time you train. Brand new novice or nationally-ranked champion, everyone brings a unique and valuable perspective if we but give them the chance to express it. You'll be pleasantly surprised by how rich that diverse experience can be.

CHAPTER TWELVE

I THOUGHT I WOULD HAVE A DOJO FULL OF FIRE-EATERS

"Spectacular achievement is always preceded by unspectacular preparation."

– Dr. Robert Schuller

Upon opening his first *dojo* in 1984, Kris had many ideas of what it would be like. Over the course of time his ideas of what should attributes the training hall should possess have changed, yet the core remains. He really wanted, and still wants, his *dojo* to be a place where people achieve, grow their martial skills and, frankly, become really proficient at karate.

For the most part those early goals are still being met, but they have taken on an unexpected flavor. The *dojo* has turned into more than just a school. It is a place where some people who have been dealt a less-than-perfect set of cards in life are able to come and participate, a safe place for them to challenge themselves and to find a little something new inside their self-concept, something that they may not have known about prior to walking through the doors.

Tim came to the *dojo* with some training under his belt. He came from a life that was way below the poverty line. He had lived there his entire existence and, further, had dropped out of high school. As his story became known around the *dojo*, there were no shaming whispers amongst the members. Instead what he got was encouragement, confirmation that he could find a better life than the one he had known.

Soon after joining Tim went began studying to earn his GED, an equivalent high school degree. Later on he worked during the day and went to school at night, putting his karate training aside for his education. He then turned his sights on the Army where he saw the potential to make a career of the military, passed the entrance exams, and off he went.

We like to think that the support he received from the people at the *dojo* made the difference, helping him realize what he could achieve, that he was not bound by the proverbial cards he had been dealt. Tim showed potential, desire, and commitment, and those happen to be the kind of attributes that most any martial arts instructor wants to foster. It's important to teach skills, but rewarding to help build character.

Making it real...

Look to those you train with and how you teach (or learn). What example are you setting? Is it punch here, kick there, or something more? Not everyone wants to change the world, but most everyone does in subtle ways whether they are trying to or not. Those changes take place one relationship at a time.

CHAPTER THIRTEEN

MY FRIEND AND HIS PHONE NUMBER

"If you already have a piece of music ingrained in your body, why would you not play it?"

– Keith Jarrett

How important are your friends? How would you know? Well, back in the days before smart phones judging a friend's importance was something that could be done by one simple test. Did you know the person's phone number? Not stored in your phone, or written down, but in your head. We used to store all the important stuff in our heads, particularly our best friends' phone numbers.

The challenge nowadays is that we rarely store information in ourselves anymore. That is bad for martial arts skills. Yup, seen it on Youtube, did it once. Seen it... sure, but can you actually do it?

Having run into this phenomenon a couple of times while working seminars, it has started to become a little more frequent in, say the last few years. Now we're not getting all judgmental here, just observational. Information is good, especially when it is transferred into wisdom. But just having information, just having seen it, being familiar with it a little—well that's not the same as ingraining it into your fiber.

Ask any person who ever wrestled, "Did you ever drill sprawls?" and the answer is going to be some form of, "Yes" followed by a grin, moan, or an eye-roll. But follow-up with the next question, "It worked for you right?" And the answer is invariably, "Yes."

Wrestlers don't just look at the sprawl and say, "Okay, got it." Wrestling coaches make sure they work it over and over again until it becomes second nature. Ask any judoka about *uchikomi*; ask any karateka about *kihon ido*. It is all the same; work it until it becomes engrained, until you can perform it flawlessly without conscious thought.

So the question this: Do you know the phone number of your best technique? Is it stored in your head or elsewhere?

Making it real...

How well do you understand your art? Can you describe the overarching strategy that makes the individual techniques succeed? If not, chances are good that it's just a collection of stuff... stuff you may or may not be able to execute under pressure when the adrenaline is flowing, say in a tournament or self-defense situation. "When does it work?" "Why does it work?" Those questions are far more important than, "How does it work?" Align strategy to tactics, know the when and why, and then you have something that's real. And usable.

CHAPTER FOURTEEN

I GOT A GOOD
FIGHT FOR YOU

""Spitting blood clears up reality and dream alike."

– Sunao

One of the brown belts comes to class and says, "Boy have I got a good fight story for you!" Randy, the brown belt who told us the story, is a plumber who primarily does outside work—digging ditches, laying pipe, that kind of stuff. Like many blue collar occupations, it's not uncommon for tempers to flare on the job site particularly during the summer when folks toil for long hours under the unrelenting heat of the sun. Well, they definitely did that day anyway.

The morning had started poorly for two of Randy's co-workers and by the afternoon the little verbal barbs had escalated into full-on "F-bombs" going both ways. It had become personal, so they decided to settle their differences with a little bout of fisticuffs. The fight was on. In one part of the client's back yard the two squared off—on one side of the small patch of lawn there was Ed, a fifty-year-old U.S. Navy veteran, and on the other side, Don, a twenty-one-year-old strapping young buck who was amped up and ready to go.

Randy said they squared off, fists up like boxers. Suddenly Ed threw the first blow, a kick to Don's right shin. With a steel-toed construction boot! Don crumpled to the ground. Ed just stood there, letting the younger man stagger back onto his feet.

"That's not fair! We're boxing!" yelled Don.

"OK," said Ed, "We'll just box now."

They squared up again, hands held high, ready to box. Pow! Ed delivered the first blow again, another shot to the shin with his steel-toed boot. Don went down once more, but this time he didn't get back up to continue the fight.

Ed, the fifty-year-old U.S. Navy veteran, could have jumped on Don while he was lying helplessly on the ground, but he didn't. He didn't need to. Ed had made his point; order was restored on the job site.

Ed had lied to Don, and Don foolishly believed him. Twice!

Rules... yeah.

Making it real...

As the proverb states, old age and treachery often trumps youth and skill. There is a time and place for a fair fight, but many, many more circumstances in which you need to stack the deck in your favor. Or, better yet, simply walk away and avoid the fight altogether. Regardless, if you have a beef with someone and then foolishly believe what they say, well let's just say that tends not to end well. Old age and treachery, indeed...

CHAPTER FIFTEEN

SMITH'S RULES
OF DESIGN #6

"Nothing is a waste of time if you use the experience wisely."

– Rodin

In the August 2008 issue of *Popular Mechanics* magazine is a great article titled, "Smith's Rules of Design." Amy Smith, who wrote it, is a senior lecturer at MIT as well as an editorial advisor to the magazine. She is a leader in the appropriate technology movement, in which engineers from developed countries work with people in the developing world to create practical, affordable solutions to everyday challenges.

The cool thing about her rules for our context is that they directly apply to martial arts... and life. We'll discuss five of them throughout this book, starting with Rule #6: "If you want to make something ten times cheaper, remove 90% of the material."

That is clear, clean stuff. It can be interpreted in two ways:

1) Cheaper means faster to make and get into operation, or

2) If you build it cheap, it's not going to last

A one-day self-defense seminar is fine, but it's also ten times cheaper. Why? Because 90% of the material has been removed. There is no history, tradition, discipline, dedication, self-exploration, and several other items. But, that doesn't mean it's not useful. It all depends on your goals.

The term "cheaper" is frequently associated with poor quality but that is not always true. If you define the item by its intended use then maybe it is not so cheap? Disposable pens, garbage bags, lighters, and other "single use" items immediately come to mind by way of example. Sure, some things should be made to last, but not everything. Imagine paying $15.00 for super-resilient, elaborately decorated garbage bag. Who in their right mind would want that?

So, cheaper isn't a problem if the end result meets your objectives. Over- or under-engineering the solution, therein lies the problem.

Making it real...

Think about what's over-engineered in your life. What aspects could you remove 90% from and find exact fit for purpose? Could you streamline training at the *dojo*? Find wiser ways to spend your time? How about giving away items you no longer need to others who might appreciate and utilize them more? Cut the clutter, focus on the essential.

CHAPTER SIXTEEN

THREE PRINCIPLES

"It is important in strategy to know the enemy's sword."

– Miyamoto Musashi

We're big fans of the philosopher Rene Descartes. We have both read much of his work (though we do not understand all of it... yet) and his biography, and have even written about him before. Even if you don't recognize his name, you probably remember his most famous quote, *cogito ergo sum*, which translates as, "I think, therefore I am."

Descartes wrote something that really applies well to the martial arts. To paraphrase, "The best government has few rules and those rules are strictly enforced."

Wow, that is some tight and deep thinking, huh? And it applies to just about everything we do when applying our discipline both in- and outside the *dojo*. Rephrased, the quote becomes, "The best martial arts have few rules and those are strictly followed."

So here is the challenge:

Find three, no more than three, guiding principles that illuminate your art, those key elements without which it simply will not work. Sounds a bit like a Monty Python joke, but more than three truly is too much. If you get it in two principles that's okay, but three is the number needed to create a pattern. There's power in that; three is the magic number.

Examples might include, "Defang the snake" as the Filipino practitioners might say. Judoka might respond, "Create imbalance." If you study Aikido, "Keep the center." Obviously that's nowhere near an all inclusive list, but hopefully it is enough to get you started.

Making it real...

It's easy to overcomplicate things when it comes to martial arts, categorizing and codifying every last detail. The challenge is that behavior tends to make things a multiple choice exercise rather than a true test of knowledge. In other words, it becomes so convoluted that in many circumstances you'll find that you cannot actually apply it successfully. Cut to the heart of the matter instead: What are the three guiding principles that you must have in order to execute your chosen art? Write them down. Discover how they are rigidly enforced. That's you're your training should be all about.

CHAPTER SEVENTEEN

KARATE & THE BEATLES

"You must research and train diligently in this."

– Miyamoto Musashi

In Kris's book, *Sanchin Kata*, he wrote about the history of the form, relating how it is likely that its true origin will never be known. We have read and seen evidence that *sanchin kata* was created and taught in China, then imported. We have also listened to Okinawan karateka explain in supremely clear and valid ways that the *sanchin kata* originated in Okinawa.

Today we have conjecture, speculation, a few pieces of history. Because of that, uncovering the true origin of the *kata* is as difficult a task as it was for ancient explorers to search and find the source of the river Nile.

Now this can be a sticky subject, who said what, and who did what before whom. Lots of rights and wrongs (like we're telling you something you have never heard before). As for us, it's really about form following function. The rest is just entertainment. We have always enjoyed history, but it is not as valuable as being able to do karate with energy and knowledge, to actually make it work in real life situations.

There's a funny video that pretends we're in the year 3,000 and archeologists have just discovered a group called *The Beatles*. It's written in jest, but it does make one wonder if this is how badly we have misunderstood events that occurred hundreds or thousands of years ago. Here's the link: http://www. maniacworld.com/beatles-1000-years-later.html

Making it real...

History of our arts, exploits of the masters who created them, it is stuff of legends. As the tales are told and retold things change—both intentionally and unintentionally. While it's good to know the history and traditions, and study the precepts of what we practice, don't get so caught up in legends that you miss out how the arts can remain relevant and be applied today.

CHAPTER EIGHTEEN

PEOPLE TIRE OF TRUTH

"I don't want any yes-men around me. I want everybody to tell me the truth even if it costs them their jobs."

– Samuel Goldwyn

It is intriguing that when people tire of an experience, a story, or an event, they have a tendency to dismiss it. The dismissal is applied across the board, almost universally to truth and falsehood alike. We get tired of stuff... and want nothing more than for it to go away.

When Kris used to work in politics (yes he was a political consultant back in the day, but he got better), he knew that most unwholesome actions of a candidate would be forgiven... if people tired of it. People would say things like, "I already know that, "or "Yeah, that's old news."

When campaign staff heard phrases like that coming from the voting population it was music to their ears. They knew that they could get over it, whatever the foible, because the voters measured issues in regard to newness, not credence. Clearly there is danger in this form of reasoning, it dismisses truth and lies equally, despite the fact that we all know they are not equal.

How does this affect us as martial artists?

Generally, we as martial artists are self-starters. We are disciplined, focused and hopefully seek truth in our training. We should seek truth and hold on to it when we find it. It does us no good to drop what we have learned in pursuit of the next shiny technique. Like an over-caffeinated five-year-old charged up with 64 oz. Mountain Dew and let loose in a Chuck E. Cheese's pizzeria is not terribly attractive, neither is chasing after the hottest new trend, jumping on the latest bandwagon, or pining over some fascinating new technique.

Bruce Lee once said, "Absorb what is useful." We would add, "...and never tire of the truth." Truth does not get old, and neither do fundaments, solid foundational techniques. By tending to and focusing on truth in our training we allow it to mature.

Making it real...

Martial arts are unique in many ways, particularly when it comes to pressure testing what you know—it either works or it doesn't. Black and white, right? Well, not really... The challenge is why it worked, or failed. Did it work because you are bigger, faster, or stronger than your opponent, because of some rule or safety limitation imposed by the drill (or tournament), or because it truly was solid stuff? Context is key; what helps you win in the ring could just as easily get you killed on the street. Seek the truth. Understand why and under what circumstances what you practice is most likely to succeed.

CHAPTER NINETEEN

BOUNDARIES

"When you live a life with no boundaries there's less joy."

– Tom Hanks

During the *Crossing the Pond Martial Expo* Al Peasland made an off-the-cuff comment to a group of participants. To paraphrase, what he said was, "Martial arts should be enjoyable. When it's not you shouldn't do it."

Al's comment made Kris think back on a moment when his martial arts training changed. Here's the story:

Sitting in the back of a car on a dim winter afternoon, three of us were heading off to our once- a-month mandatory workout at the regional *dojo*. These workouts had begun as an impromptu get-together, a chance to work on techniques, standardize some things, and have a little fellowship time. All of those things were good things, of course, but the tone had changed after we'd met a few times when the head instructor suddenly began calling these sessions "mandatory" meetings.

Leaning forward from the back seat I listened to the two other black belts talking. I can't recall the whole conversation, but one phrase absolutely gut-punched me. The driver, who I respect for his intelligence and insight, said, "Mandatory! There's nothing mandatory when it comes to my karate. I do this because I like it, not because I'm told to."

The metaphorical gut-punch made me sit back into the darkness of the back seat. I wish I could say that, at that moment, I came to an epiphany but I didn't. All I had was the realization that I had given away my sovereignty.

I felt the fool.

I had considered myself to be in charge of my own destiny; however the realization that I had this enormous blind-spot didn't sit well with my ego one bit. Over the next couple of months I came to the conclusion that I was not going to give up my sovereignty anymore. I decided I would engage in the martial arts on my terms. I was going to say, "No thank you" more often. My training was now going to be totally my own I was going to be responsible for what I worked, what I studied, and let the chips fall where they may.

Call it boundaries if you like.

Making it real...

The relationship between students and teachers is complex, especially in the field of martial arts where instructors may hold a higher-degree of power over their students than in other disciplines. While a math or science teacher can flunk you, a martial arts instructor can literally kill you. History and traditions of the arts make it easy for malevolent *sensei* to manipulate, subjugate, or even abuse students who blindly follow their directives. Consequently such relationships need to be founded on trust, integrity, and honesty. Think about your relationship with your instructor(s). Is it professional and positive or, like the proverbial frog in the boiling pot, have you given away your sovereignty, hence need to reestablish boundaries.

CHAPTER TWENTY

THINGS GET VERY STILL

"The ordinary person concerned with self-defense has a job that is easier than the professional's in some ways and harder in others. Being mindful of one's surroundings takes additional effort and skill, beyond that required in one's daily life. For the professional, that is one's daily life."

– Jack M. Feldman

Martin Scorsese, the director of *Taxi Driver*, *Raging Bull*, and *Goodfellas*, to name a few famous movies, told Miguel Arteta, the director of *Youth in Revolt*, that when you want to show the audience that violence is about to happen things get very still. Don't move the camera.

Life is often like that. When somebody is about to become violent they will often get very still, and then suddenly explode into the violence. It doesn't always happen that way, of course, but like most stereotypes it is common enough in reality that we have come to expect such things on the silver screen.

Scorsese is a master of his craft. His movies and accolades show that he knows how to touch us with his filmmaking. The way he does it is by using common experience.

Common environment is not necessary, yet common experience is required for us to connect to, hence believe, what we're seeing on film. Using fear, hatred, love, and betrayal, Scorsese reaches out and meet us with these experiences. It's why he's so good at what he does. This meeting of commonality allows him to bring us emotionally into a foreign environment, to find empathy with a mobster or a boxer, even when we know nothing of the character's world.

So when you watch for violence, look toward what real-life says. And, listen to what one of the greatest directors of all time pointed out... when violence is about to happen things get very still.

Making it real...

Ponder some of the greatest violent scenes you have seen in film and you will see that Scorsese is right. Now, review the violence you have seen or experienced in real life or, if you've been lucky enough to avoid confrontation your entire existence, spend a little time on YouTube. You'll see that Scorsese is correct there as well. To have good situational awareness you don't necessarily have to spot all the tiny precursors of violence, you just need to identify the change of energy, the proverbial calm before the storm. Notice the stillness, pay attention, and take action to keep yourself safe.

CHAPTER TWENTY-ONE

THE DUNNING-KRUGER EFFECT

"Ignorance constitutes our peace of mind; self-deception our felicity."

– Anatole France

Years ago when Kris first began teaching karate at the YMCA and Lawrence became his student, Billy Blanks Tae Bo fitness was all the rage. Heading to class each night we would spot a gym full of some 80+ people doing Tae Bo, three times the number who attended karate class. And, everybody in the Tae Bo class was kicking and punching themselves into a frenzy.

After the class broke-up one night a young gal spotted Kris in his karate *gi*, walked over to him and said, "That's a great work out."

"Yeah it sure looks like it," he replied, acknowledging the sweat dripping down her face.

"It feels great to know that I can finally defend myself," she continued.

Kris didn't say a word, just smiled and nodded acknowledgment that she'd spoken. Internally he was stunned by the boldness of her declaration. To karate practitioners, the idea that Tae Bo was anything more than a fitness routine was laughable, but for a student who had no way of knowing better it was something more.

Guess what? That young lady's comment and unrealistically high sense of ability is called The Dunning-Kruger Effect. Here's how it works: People reach false conclusions about their abilities based on how they feel, not facts. Further their inability to analyze their skill doesn't allow them to see their lack of ability. This lack of internal analysis lets them believe that they are really on top of something, even to the point of rating themselves above others who truly are competent.

The Dunning-Kruger effect is actually a two-edged sword, one that deeply cuts both ways. It is based on an error about one's own abilities, and then it gets compounded by an internal knowledge that the person is better than those who are truly competent. Wow, delusional thinking explained by the Dunning-Kruger, have to remember that...

There is a quote from Bertrand Russell, a British Philosopher and Mathematician amongst other things, about the confident. It goes, "The trouble with the world is that the stupid are cocksure and the intelligent are full of doubt."

At the end of the day, people who experience the Dunning-Kruger Effect are happy people. Just like that gal who believed that the Tae Bo class finally gave her an understanding of physical defenses, as well as a set of combat skills, the rest of us will be over here going through our own happy, and slightly neurotic, never-ending explorations of the arts.

Making it real...

The good news is that by living in modern society where laws and legal systems hold sway, most of us will never have our bubble burst by finding out the hard way that what we think we know doesn't actually work. The bad news is that martial artists who find themselves in such situations often struggle to deal with the psychological impact of the aftermath, let alone any physical recover or rehabilitation. Better to find out by pressure-testing our skills in a controlled environment than to allow the Dunning-Kruger effect to leave us happily self-deceived. If you haven't already done so, seek out such opportunities and discover where you truly stand. That doesn't necessarily mean changing your training in any way, but rather having a realistic appraisal of where you stand.

CHAPTER TWENTY-TWO

The Old Man Medici

"An ostentatious man will rather relate a blunder or an absurdity he has committed, than be debarred from talking of his own dear person."

– Joseph Addison

The Medici family was one of if not the most influential household in Italy for some 400 years. They amassed great fortunes and wielded enormous power. How much wealth and power? Oh, enough to start a bank... and to have one member of the family become Pope back in the days where that title ranked above kings, among other things. That kind of power.

They lived elite lives that only the superrich could afford, owing multiple houses, servants, and lands, their gold-embossed, hand-painted family portraits hanging on the walls of palatial estates. Just about whatever your mind can conceive of for that time, they did... and then some.

The first Medici, Averardo de' Medici, was the one that is most interesting of the clan. Although wealthy, he rode a donkey and dressed in average clothing when out doing his business of the day. His home showed little outward markings of opulence and he suggested that everyone else in his family do the same. Why, you might ask? The reason for his policy was simple; he wanted to fly under the proverbial radar, didn't want to become the target of thieves, kidnappers, or other criminals.

In Averardo's world, he felt no need to be a peacock. It was safer for him to look like a common bird. Further Averardo wielded power quietly, without any ostentatious displays, yet from behind the scenes he pulled strings at the highest levels. Sometimes real power does not need to be flaunted; it needs to be held close to the vest until needed.

Making it real...

Follow the de' Medici example by living low. A modern illustration of this could be the federal air marshal. Lawrence travels a lot on business. Oftentimes there is an armed air marshal on his flights, yet few if any passengers know that he or she is there. Taking a page from Alvarado de' Medici's playbook, the marshals keep their skills hidden until, or unless, they are needed. Live simply in public. Don't be a peacock who struts around in an ostentatious *dogi* with a gaggle of hangers on calling you "master" day and night. What worked in Medici's day works equally well if not better today.

CHAPTER TWENTY-THREE

Bad Authority

"Every revolution evaporates and leaves behind only the slime of a new bureaucracy."

– Franz Kafka

Lawrence turned to Kris one day and said, "You have a real problem with authority, don't you?"

Kris replied, "Not really. I have a problem with bad authority."

It's true. We both have a problem with bad authority, actually.

How do we define bad authority? Quite simply it's slavish compliance to process to the exclusion of the actual goal. We all have seen numerous examples of this bureaucracy in our lives—whenever we are forced to deal with banks, insurance companies, licensing agencies, schools, government institutions, or the like.

If there's a form to fill out, chances are good there's bad authority at play.

It's fun to make fun of bureaucracy, right? And far too easy most days, primarily because of bureaucracy's slavish devotion to process irrespective of any actual goal—such as solving your problem. Bureaucrats tend to create inflexible rules that must be implemented by un-empowered drones in the most inefficient way possible (what, us cynical?).

Comedian Shelly Berman deftly demonstrates that inefficient bureaucracy is the equivalent of dealing with a child in the following clip: http://www.youtube.com/watch?v=nWwUgjkOHAA

Making it real...

We might not be able to control bureaucracy levied upon us, but we absolutely can control what we force others to endure. And, of course, what burdens we place upon ourselves. What is your ultimate goal of your art? Carve, chip, and whittle it down to one sentence, "The purpose of my martial arts is_____." Now reflecting on the mission statement you've just written, see how it matches up with what you are doing whenever you train. Are you slavishly devoted to process, or are you working toward a worthwhile accomplishment?

CHAPTER TWENTY-FOUR

CHALLENGING PLAYGROUNDS

"Take calculated risks. That is quite different from being rash."

– George S. Patton

Comedian Bill Cosby did a now-classic comedy bit years ago about how the playgrounds at parks were deliberately designed by adults to kill and maim children. Cosby then went on to make fun of each one of the playground toys and demonstrate their maniacally ingenious design.

Comedy aside, these playgrounds were challenging. For example, the steel slides became intensely hot in the summertime. The lesson: "Look before you leap." You only got on that slide once in your shorts before realizing it was a really bad idea. Heck, in a feat of eight-year-old ingenuity we used to pour water down the slide to cool it off before using it.

The Merry-Go-Round... What did we learn from the Merry-Go-Round? Going too fast will hurl you off onto the asphalt which hurts like heck and a half. Chalk that one up in the column of "Going too fast is a bad thing." The monkey bars, oh the life-lessons contained on the monkey bars. Important stuff like, "At the halfway point, you need to push on because trying to go backward is too hard. And, falling hurts."

Life lesson #16: "Failure hurts more than diligence."

Today the slides are made of plastic. The Merry-Go-Round now has some sort of space-age polymer bouncy stuff surrounding it to eliminate road-rash and other injuries. The Monkey Bars are now lowered so that most kids can just stand underneath and reach up with no threat of the dreaded three-foot drop. Teeter-totters? They're banned outright at most playgrounds. Oh, and don't forget the ubiquitous sawdust and padded surfaces all around.

What sorts of lessons are being learned nowadays? Where are the stitches, the scabs?

Look, we're parents. We're certainly not advocating the maiming of our youth, but the playground ought to be a place where skills and life experiences are honed. Look at nature; play amongst mammals is critical to maturation and skill development. In every species it helps prepare youngsters for adulthood. An overabundance of safety keeps people from learning.

Making it real...

As adults we know that the world is full of hard, hot surfaces that will hurt us if we are not wary. So, to bring this topic back around to the martial arts school, shouldn't those of us who teach be creating a challenging playground where we can smile, laugh, have fun, gain a little wisdom, and maybe get a bruise or two? We sure think so. Be safe, but don't over-rotate. Pain is your friend; injury not so much...

CHAPTER TWENTY-FIVE

15 MINUTES AND 30 YEARS

"Try not to become a man of success but rather to become a man of value."

– Albert Einstein

We buy our *gi*s from Kensho International. It is a company owned and run by Mike O'Donnell. Mike is one of the good guys. He teaches karate, is a small businessman, and makes some of the finest hand-crafted *kobudo* weapons on the planet.

Kris is the one who picks up the orders. He and Mike talk about everything under the sun while they walk from room to room filling the orders. One afternoon Mike started talking about an artist he met who makes the most realistic watercolor paintings he had ever seen. As they progressed to his office to complete the paperwork Mike quipped that the painting, "Wasn't cheap, either." He went further, "I asked him (the artist) how long did take to make that painting?"

The artist replied, just as Mike suspected he would, and in a creative way. "15 minutes and 30 years," he said smiling back at Mike.

We'll do the math... 15 minutes, divided by $10,000 dollars equals $666.66 per minute. By most accounts that's an outrageous amount! If we measure it by the 30 years, on the other hand, the cost of the painting becomes: 1 year = 525,948 minutes x 30 years = 15,778,400 minutes. $10,000 / 15,778,400 minutes = $0.00063 per minute. The result is an hourly wage that even the neediest individual from the most backwards third world country you can think of would likely refuse, $0.037 cents.

For the record Mike, as a master woodworker was in on the joke. He wanted to see how the watercolor artist expressed his value. And, was pleased with the answer.

Shihan John Roseberry has a quote from his teacher, Seikichi Toguchi, on the wall of his *dojo* that says, "A teacher gives the student his life, the student gives the teacher his spare time." So there it is. A painter and a martial artist giving you two ways to express the value of what we do as practitioners. Count it one way and the arts are virtually worthless. Measure it another way and their value is extraordinary.

Making it real...

How is your value measured? How do you measure the value of your teacher? Is the calculation based on 15 minutes or 30 years? If asked the same question, what would your students think? Most importantly, is there anything you'd change based on that response? If so, there's no time like the present to correct your course.

CHAPTER TWENTY-SIX

BE AWARE... PFFFT...
USELESS

"By staying alert and reporting any problems on buses or at bus stops and shelters, you can help make Metro Transit safer, friendlier and better for everyone."

— Public Safety Partnership

"Be aware!" Pffft... useless. It's said in a variety of different ways, "Be aware," "Don't get hit," "Stay alert," "Pay attention;" whatever the explanation there's near universal agreement amongst martial arts instructors that the first principle of self-defense is discerning and avoiding threats before you have to fight. Lawrence likes to say, "Self defense isn't about fighting. Fighting is what you do once you've blown your self-defense."

Okay, we all get it. Good situational awareness keeps you safe. The challenge is that in most instances the way this principle is presented is utterly useless. Folks need more than platitudes, they need to understand what awareness is, what it's not, and more importantly how to implement it in a manner that's actually useful. Clearly we cannot walk about like crazed meth-heads flinching at every moth that goes zigzagging past use on its way to the nearest light.

Assuming that every person who passes within arm's-length in every public place is a threat is not going to work either. Sorry, but we're not going to throw down on grandma while standing in line at the Safeway pharmacy just because we can't see what's in her hands. No upside.

As self-defense instructors we are always seeking ways to condense, to distill our methodologies down into actionable statements that others can make use of. How does one assemble the idea of being aware?

Well, one of the best answers we've heard came from a law enforcement officer named Ivan. He said, "The cop has the job of investigating the unusual."

We do that all the time subconsciously, all humans do, but being aware that we are looking for the unusual is the kicker. Our instincts, honed through thousands of years of evolution, are awful good at spotting threats, but for the vast majority (in the developed world), this survival instinct has been conditioned out of us. We get into the elevator with that creepy stranger because we don't want to seem rude. Been there, done that, right? Most times it doesn't matter, nothing bad happens, but every so often ignoring our survival signals can become a very serious matter.

For example, when Lawrence worked security at a college football stadium there was a vendor who everybody called, "Creepy Popcorn Guy." He certainly was creepy and he sold popcorn... to kids. Despite the fact that everyone who encountered this individual had a gut-level reaction, they all assumed he'd passed a background check hence did not act on their intuition. One day Lawrence became concerned and decided to check. Long story short, somehow this guy's paperwork had gotten lost. When the background check was performed the administration discovered they had inadvertently hired a Level 3 sex offender who preyed on children. Creepy Popcorn Guy was subsequently arrested for violating his probation.

Being actively aware that you are looking for anomalies in pattern makes a tremendous difference in the identification and assessment of threats. It bolsters you to take action when something pings your intuition. Ask anyone who does crowd control, works a door, bounces, or enforces laws for a living and they will tell you that they look for the disturbances. Anything not "normal," unusual patterns, sights, sounds, or smells warrants attention. Once they've identified that a disturbance has taken place then they can figure out why it is unusual and determine whether or not any action on their part is warranted.

Of course the professional's job is to move toward the disturbance, tackling danger, whereas a civilian's is to move the other way and remain safe. Either way, it's the anomaly that tips us off, allowing us to prepare to act.

Condensing these ideas to a (hopefully) useful maxim, we get, "Know the baseline, listen to your instincts, and pay extra attention to anything abnormal."

Making it real...

In many ways situational awareness is far easier to practice than it is to explain. Does our maxim work for you? If not, what's your version? Take a few minutes and write it down, then see if you can successfully make it clear to someone else. Viscerally understanding awareness helps make it actionable.

CHAPTER TWENTY-SEVEN

LAWS OF NATURE & THE CROSSWALK

"Pardon him, Theodotus. He is a barbarian and thinks that the customs of his tribe and island are the laws of nature."

– George Bernard Shaw

If you drive through a large city enough you wind up spotting interesting things. For example, fools who believe that, "I am safe when I am in this crosswalk" and act accordingly. How many times have you seen a young man or woman texting, never even looking up let alone to either side as they step into the crosswalk? Like a bunch of lemmings they simply respond to the "walk" light (or in some instances bleating signal) and jump out in between the lines of magically protective white paint.

Got news for you bubba, paint lines don't keep you safe.

We all know that crosswalk guy has all the rules, laws, and rights on his side. He is 100% justified in walking into that crosswalk once the light has changed. Those are the laws of man. The laws of nature, on the other hand, say that if a driver doesn't see or chooses to ignore that light for any reason whatsoever, dude in the crosswalk will be on the receiving end of a half-ton of hurling steel and fiberglass. That's a losing proposition if ever there was one. We'd have to say that the laws of nature trump the laws of man every single time in such instances.

The point of the previous chapter on awareness was that we cannot go around on high alert all the time. It's not healthy and, frankly, not possible. Nevertheless, situational alertness is a darn good idea. So let's solve this problem with a quote from former U.S. President Ronald Reagan, "Trust but verify." This is a great maxim to use not only in world affairs, but also in martial arts, and our day-to-day lives too.

You use it on the *dojo* floor already don't you? For example, in sparring you have a follow-up technique primed and ready to go if your first application fails, right? You follow through on a throw, punch, or kick, not just stand there passively and see what happens. Sure, you trust that your technique will work, but if your opponent disrupts your plans you pull something new out of your bag of tricks and give it a try.

The main message here is the laws of nature trump the laws any government can promulgate. Trust in the law, you're one of the good guys right? But don't be so blind as to think that everyone else follows them too.

So we guess the maxim now reads; "Honor nature's laws while looking for abnormal behavior." Yeah, nice maxim that bookends the two extremes.

"Be Aware!" Pffft... useless. Oh wait, we already said that...

Making it real...

Most martial artists are law abiding citizens. Far too many of us automatically assume that those we interact with share the same values. Let's face the facts, however, laws are just pieces of paper written by folks who have no skin in the game at the moment when things go south in our interactions with others. And not just between good guys and bad guys—we've all seen otherwise good people act foolishly due to distraction, inattention, altered states of consciousness, or whatever. Do drunk, high, or distracted drivers intend to kill people? Almost certainly not, but they take people out every single day. So, at risk of beating a dead horse, pay attention! Make a vow not to listen to music, text, daydream, or otherwise lose track of your surroundings whenever you're moving around in public. Pay attention, and if something feels wrong be prepared to act. It's no nirvana, but it's definitely a good start.

CHAPTER TWENTY-EIGHT

FOOD ALLERGIES MAKE KIDS A TARGET OF BULLIES

"When a resolute young fellow steps up to the great bully, the world, and takes him boldly by the beard, he is often surprised to find it comes off in his hand, and that it was only tied on to scare away the timid adventurers."

– Ralph Waldo Emerson

The End... it's officially here.

Apparently food allergies now make kids a target of bullies... This is what we have come to? Apparently it's a big enough story that Anderson Cooper did a special edition of his show on Food Bullies and CNN printed an article on the same subject. We have included a few excerpts from CNN article below and posted the link at the end of this chapter so that you can find it if you really want to waste your time reading all the gory details.

"He said [he was] scared, and 'sad that he would do that to me,' and 'mad that he would do that to me,' and worried that it's going to happen again," the boy's mother told reporters.

"...doctors are becoming more conscious of a disturbing trend in children getting picked on for not being able to eat certain foods."

"The school has to really address it. It's not the child's job to take care of this problem, because there is already an imbalance of power..."

What, the f&#@... ?! That is what bullies do. They freaking bully people!!! If you are different or weak, you are a target. It's just that simple. Always has been and likely always will be.

We don't care if the entire European Union, China, and the Western Hemisphere craft an anti-bully policy and have it tattooed on every child's forehead, bullies will still exist. Bullies existed before this special group of food-allergic kids became victims and bullies will exist after all of us are gone from this earth. Bullies and cockroaches... welcome to the apocalypse.

We'll venture a guess that at least half the people reading this book began practicing the martial arts to deal with some bully issue. Lawrence did; after getting picked-on as a kid his dad sent him to *Sensei* Yamada to learn how to man up. Guess what, it worked too. Of course there weren't any "zero tolerance" polices way back then, so he was able to deal with his bully problem a bit more directly than is possible nowadays. Regardless, it led to his lifelong interest in the martial arts.

How many of you were in the same boat? Feels pretty good to steer your own way out of the bully mess doesn't it?

All problems can't be solved by fighting, but those who are able to fight tend to have a lot less problems. A solid martial arts program builds confidence, mental and physical strength, discipline, and an enhanced sense of self worth. All-in-all, that's a pretty good recipe for fending off potential bullies regardless of whether they're honed in on food allergies or anything else.

For those who want to read the article we referenced in its entirety, here's the link: http://www.cnn.com/2010/HEALTH/09/28/food.allergy.bullying/?hpt=T2

Making it real...

If we were talking to folks whose children are victims of food allergy bullies, or at risk of getting picked on for being different in any way, we'd tell them to get their kid into martial arts. Or just about any sport, for that matter. Physical activities will create a sense of accomplishment and self-worth that can never be granted by decree. Whether you're a martial arts student or teacher, sooner or later you'll run across a child who could use your help, help to build the confidence necessary not only to circumnavigate bullies but also to succeed in life. When you get that opportunity lend a hand.

CHAPTER TWENTY-NINE

SIMPLICITY

"Simplicity is the peak of civilization."

– Jessie Sampter

Lawrence recently overheard a guy talking about one of his college professors who complained to the students that their papers where full of fluff. He told them that they spent too much effort in filling the mandated number of pages without ever saying anything meaningful. Interesting how little certain things change over time. Lawrence heard that same complaint from a different professor a little over 30 years ago, only that time he was one of the students being lectured.

The human mind seems to love complexity, but is complexity necessary? Nature builds diversity from a series of simple commands. In fact, much of what appears to be complex is really just a compounding of simple components.

Neither of us are fans of complexity, especially not in the martial arts. We're pretty sure that much of what is commonly observed in training is nothing more than machinations designed to titillate the mind— sorta like a bright fishing lure used to hook a tout. Unneeded complexity.

Frankly, simplicity and efficiency go hand-in-hand (refer back to nature once again). Complexity breaks down under pressure. The last things we need in a fight are fragile martial arts techniques. We want simple, vigorous, and dependable "go to" applications, ones that work no matter how much dexterity or intellect we give up to adrenaline and fear.

Not buying our argument? Here's a proof point. World renowned judo champion Yamashita was famous for using *o-soto gari*, one of the first learned and most basic throws of judo canon to win. And win he certainly did... in spades. Here's a list:

- 85 All-Japan Championships – Tokyo, Japan
- 84 Olympic Games (Open) – Los Angeles, CA, USA
- 84 All-Japan Championships – Tokyo, Japan
- 83 World Championships (+95kg) – Moscow, Russia
- 83 All-Japan Championships – Tokyo, Japan
- 82 All-Japan Championships – Tokyo, Japan
- 81 World Championships (+95kg & Open) – Maastricht, Holland

- 81 All-Japan Championships – Tokyo, Japan
- 80 All-Japan Championships – Tokyo, Japan
- 79 World Championships (+95kg) – Paris, France
- 79 All-Japan Championships – Tokyo, Japan
- 78 All-Japan Championships – Tokyo, Japan
- 77 All-Japan Championships – Tokyo, Japan

Pretty impressive for a guy who relied on a simple, basic technique, huh? As Alexander Pope once wrote, "There is a certain majesty in simplicity." It seems to us that *o-soto gari* exemplifies that thought, especially in the way Yamashita was able to use it.

Thanks to Neil Ohlenkamp at http://judoinfo.com/yamashita.htm for the preceding list of Yamashita's championships.

Making it real...

Simplicity and efficiency, now that's a great mantra! So here's your challenge: Choose a part of your art and dive down deep into that aspect to find the simple core. For example, controlling the opponent's center of gravity—that's key for throws, sweeps, and takedowns. Once you have found that simple core, practice it every day for the next month. Look back afterward and consider how much you learned by abandoning the complex and focusing on simplicity.

CHAPTER THIRTY

YOUR OWN SENSE OF SUCCESS

"At the end of the day, the goals are simple: Safety and security."

– Jodi Rell

Practicing martial arts for nearly eighty years combined, we have come in contact with a lot of practitioners, folks from all walks of life. The people who come into the *dojo* have ranged from work-a-day Joe's, to executives, small business owners, teachers, and parents. Heck, we've trained with folks who have held pretty much any occupation you can think of. And, we have learned that none of these people were satisfied with their lives unless and until they had developed their own sense of success, an internal guidance system based on their values.

If you are going to define your success externally, by how other people see you, you are never going to fill in that giant hole called ultimate success. There is not enough dirt in the world to fill it up. When you define your own ways of success, however then what happens is that you become a unique brand unto yourself. You are an individual. One of the greatest desires for man, and by that we mean "man" is a race not as a gender, is to be what author Tom Wolfe called "A man in full."

Loren Christensen, a prolific author, retired cop, martial artist, and all around decent guy, once told us that his definition of success was, "Being able to come home safely and watch Johnny Carson every night." While working as a law enforcement officer he knew that he had completed a successful shift when he was in bed watching Johnny instead of cleaning up some horrific mess that used to be a human being, wading through mountains of paperwork, or being patched-up in the emergency room. That was how Loren measured success—simple, clean, and goal-oriented.

Making it real...

When it comes to your martial art, do you make it personal? Do you define what success looks like or do you allow others to do it for you? In the early stages of your martial journey perhaps it makes sense to have others meter your progress, show you the way, but the end game is always your own. Ruminate on what success looks like, write it down, and then look back on what you've written in a month, a year. If something's changed, ask yourself why.

CHAPTER THIRTY-ONE

PURE BREEDS AND MUTTS

"I used to be Snow White, but I drifted."

– Mae West

When Kris was a kid his family lived on a farm. When you live on a farm, pretty much everything lying around has to be useful. Everything has to contribute. Their family car was a station wagon. That vehicle not only ferried around his parents, himself, and his brother, but it also carried feed and animals too. Lots of utility.

Dogs were an important part of farm life. The family's two dogs served as guards, keeping coyotes away from the chickens. They also made great doorbells whenever somebody pulled into the driveway. And, when Kris was a kid they were great playmates too. Neither of these dogs were purebreds, they where mutts, admixtures of Beagle, Airedale, and German Sheppard all swirled together with who knows what all else.

When Kris asked his dad one day why they didn't have purebreds, just mutts, his answer was simple, "Purebred dogs have problems." He went on to explain about how some purebreds had hip problems, others digestive issues, and the behaviors that were bred into them were not always what was best for a good farm dog.

His point was that the temperament and resiliency of the mutt was well suited for the rigors of the farm, useful and low maintenance. Kind of like the family station wagon. Further they were nice dogs with good personalities, dependable, easy to acquire, and cheap to maintain.

Making it real...

Here's your audit: If your martial art was a dog, would it be a mutt or a purebred? Is your martial arts school the Westminster dog show, or is it a working farm? We submit to you that the purebred art is just like the purebred dog, looks great, but not particularly durable and in the final conclusion not horribly useful either.

CHAPTER THIRTY-TWO

TELL BRUCE LEE
IT HAPPENED

"Tell 'em to God. Don' go burdenin' other people with your sins. That ain't decent."

– John Steinbeck

We recall that Bruce Lee saying something along the lines of not wanting to live to be an old man. That's paraphrasing, obviously, we don't remember the exact quote, but we're far more interested in the idea he conveyed than his exact words anyway.

The point of Lee's comment was that he didn't want to live a diminished life. We assume he was saying that he wanted to live life on his terms and not be a burden, become dependent upon others. Now we can discuss what he meant by his comment, parse out the nuance, or change the context, but just bear with us for a moment and let us take the comment for what it looks like on the surface, because taking what Lee said at face value brings us to the question of, "When it happened?"

"When what happened," you ask. When did the zeitgeist of our culture change from "can do!" and ready for risk to "I am owed [insert something here]"? When did people decide that it was better to live a much longer, yet unchallenged life? When did people decide that there is no need to get up and get it done, back when the "it" was something worth doing?

Kris has an acquaintance who he is required to come into contact with fairly often. This man announces, doesn't just work it into the conversation, but actually announces on a regular basis that he is, "On disability." In every conversation! This syndrome isn't just limited to one man either. It seems as if people regularly seek out distinct classifications for their diminished capacities... and they are rewarded for doing so.

Don't get us wrong, we sincerely wish for all folks with disabilities to live rich, full lives. This chapter isn't about beating up on the disabled. What we're railing against here are the ones who hang it on their sleeve, wave it in your face, and proudly leach off the welfare/charity of others. Many of them aren't unable to work, they're unwilling. Somehow in the last few decades far too many individuals have gone from unleashing their creative energies to relishing indolence.

So here is Bruce Lee saying that he doesn't want to be a burden. Lee wanted to live life on his own terms. On the other side of the equation is a whole stratum of our society that seeks a sense of themselves and a trivial bounty from the powers that be, which strives to actually eke out a diminished life.

What's up with that?

Making it real...

What's your contribution? In what ways do you plan to leave the world a better place than you found it? Is it by being a good employee, a great parent, a brilliant teacher? What mark do you want to leave? And, more importantly, what are you doing to make it happen?

CHAPTER THIRTY-THREE

PERFECT LIGHT AND MAKEUP

"My psychiatrist told me I was crazy and I said I want a second opinion. He said okay, you're ugly too."

– Rodney Dangerfield

Among other things, Lawrence is a reporter. He uses his press card to get the "best seat in the house" during our son's high school football games where he works as a sideline photographer, publishing pictures not only for the team but also for local news agencies. A big challenge he faces is that high school stadiums have notoriously poor lighting, making it extremely difficult to get crisp, clean shots during the fast action even with a high end camera and lens. One of the tools he's found for making photos meet the expected, professional standards for publication is Adobe Photoshop.

For those who don't already know, Photoshop is a powerful computer program used to edit and enhance pictures. It's amazing what it can do. In addition to adjusting lighting, exposure, and the like, Photoshop can be used to enhance what you have photographed, say removing bags from under celebrities' eyes.

The changes that can be made with Photoshop are virtually unlimited. Crow's feet disappear, complexion clears, skin tones change, and suddenly an average-looking individual becomes a glamorous model. Posing a model under the perfect, soft artificial lights of a portrait studio makes a world of difference. Having an experienced professional doing the set-up and camerawork adds another level of illusion to the equation as there are in-camera tricks, filters, shooting angles, and the like that can make just about any scene turn out exactly how you want it.

Here, is a link to a minute and a half video showing the power of make-up and Photoshop: http://www.youtube.com/watch?v=iYhCn0jf46U&feature=related

All of these items, camera tricks, software, plastic surgery, and the like contribute to the whole illusion, and that is what it is, illusion. We might say, "I know it isn't real," but our minds don't truly know or our subconscious's believe it. We accept far too much without question because our minds don't audit the process initially, they just makes an assessment, good or bad, threat or non-threat, that sort of thing.

So when we see the illusion, we tend to accept it without scrutiny.

Go back and look at the 0:50 mark of the video we referenced, the spot where the picture goes onto a billboard. Look at her neck—it is elongated, but not so much as to be abnormal, just not real. Now you might also notice that when you looked at the picture originally you didn't analyze it, you accepted it even knowing that her neck had been changed.

"OK," you say, "Where is this going?"

Well, let us extend the Photoshop metaphor: Violence is ugly, it rarely goes as planned, and an elegant *dojo* solution is not likely to withstand the pressure of effective and swift violence on the street.

Well all know that intellectually, but few "get it" viscerally. Consequently we suggest that if not careful a *dojo* can turn into a form of martial arts Photoshop, a room with perfect light, governed by a professional enrobed in authority, dictating and guiding the process. And, turning it into an illusion...

Look, we're not dissing the *dojo* experience. Good grief, Kris runs a *dojo* and Lawrence teaches there! It takes effort and a keen eye to ensure that the *dojo* retains the metaphorical crow's feet and bags under the eyes, call it an attempt to keep it real... while, of course, being safe.

Don't fall for the illusion.

Making it real...

All drills in the *dojo* have flaws, built in safety features designed to let us practice with intensity yet go home in one piece afterward. These flaws are important, and good, but sometimes we forget they exist. Then they become a very bad thing. Whenever you do a drill, make a conscious effort to point out the flaw. Say it out loud. Are you going slower? Removing certain targets? Using a willing opponent? Adding safety gear? Whatever it is, point out the intentional flaw. Simply knowing it's there helps add a level realism, assuring that you aren't setting yourself for failure if you ever have to use what you've practiced on the street.

CHAPTER THIRTY-FOUR

TELL BRUCE LEE, ALL IS NOT LOST

"Patience and perseverance have a magical effect before which difficulties disappear and obstacles vanish."

– John Quincy Adams

There is just a large metaphorical canyon in today's world. This canyon has a rapidly flowing, boulder-strewn river, craggy, steep canyon walls, poisonous snakes and carnivores of all sizes roam within, and strong winds separate the sides. On one side of this canyon are the folks who proudly declare their infirmities and find power via a codification of everything "wrong" with them. On the other side of this canyon are a different species of person, yeah we use the word species because they are not the same critter. These people have crossed the canyon, moved past it, and are pushing onward.

Despite challenges, there are many who have pushed on to the other side of the canyon. And several of them have passed though our *dojo* door. One guy who comes into the *dojo* who can't eat solid food, oh and he has multiple sclerosis too. We like this guy a lot and his demeanor belies the struggles that he has to go through every day. He has a steadiness, an outlook on life that we're not sure we could muster under the same conditions.

Another student has cerebral palsy. Another needs special hearing aids, and he is six years old. And then still another is legally blind without his glasses.

One of our students was killed by his disease. He would sleep during the day so he could save his energy for class. He did this until his liver literally disintegrated, falling apart inside his own body and causing him to bleed to death. A few days before that happened he was working alongside us in the *dojo*.

These folks are examples for us. Their courage and perseverance leave us speechless. Some people just blow us away with the way they can will the disparate aspects of their lives into one cohesive focus... and we are fortunate and blessed to come into contact with them.

Did you know:

- Ludwig van Beethoven was deaf
- Thomas Edison, Albert Einstein, Woodrow Wilson (U.S. President), all were Dyslexic

- ♦ Stephen Hawking, is addled by Lou Gehrig's disease

- ♦ John F. Kennedy had Addison's disease, an adrenal insufficiency

- ♦ Sir Winston Churchill, Clara Barton, and Carly Simon we all stutterers

- ♦ Homer, the Greek Poet, he was blind

So go tell Bruce Lee that not all is lost. However he needs to know there are two types of people in the world. One group stands on the canyon edge looking at the insurmountable obstacles that block their path. The others have crossed despite all the dangers and are pushing on toward their future.

Oh, and did you know that one of Bruce Lee's legs was shorter than the other? And it didn't stop him.

Did you know we all have one leg shorter than the other?

It is all in how you measure, how you choose to see yourself in the world.

Hey Bruce, all is not lost!

Making it real...

What do you want to do when you grow up? Seriously. Whatever your age, whatever your station, there's something you still want to do, right? What is it? And, how do you plan to get there? As the old saying goes, people seldom hit what they do not aim for. Given the right opportunity, most people step up (or sadly down) to expectations. Setting lofty yet achievable goals for yourself and those in your charge affords an opportunity to grow. For best results make sure that they are specific, measurable, achievable, relevant, and time-bound too.

CHAPTER THIRTY-FIVE

STREET KIDS AND THE DOJO

"The greatest gift that you can give to others is the gift of unconditional love and acceptance."

– Brian Tracy

A phone call came in a while back from a friendly guy named Scott. Scott works with a group called New Horizon Ministries, folks who work with street kids and at-risk youth. Scott wanted to know if Kris would do a class or two for the street kids. Probably goes without saying, but the answer was yes.

These kids showed up and piled out of the van. They dove straight in to the *dojo*, loud and full of grins. Shoes and socks come off. I watch them cram unwashed socks into boots and shoes. "Hand-up, your coats," I say. Dirty coats get put away removing the protective sealant that contains their... what could be best called "hobo funk."

As the class develops these kids start to exhibit some impressive skills of observation, mimicry and a remarkable array of knowledge crossing many disinclines. These kids are impressive, streetwise, quick, direct, and bold in their opinions. They know how to take a conversation and make it theirs, make it useful to them. Their naiveté is also blinding. Their lives are all about experience and resource there is little thought beyond the immediate future.

One kid says, "I like this, how much does it cost to train here?"

"More than you have, let's just work on this now." I reply.

"Oh I got ways to get money." He says.

"You can't do weed, or sell weed and train here, no drugs."

"Oh," he says, and slowly re-enters the ongoing drill.

That conversation ends.

"Come over here," I say. I start calling out sizes and handing out karate shirts to the kids. Their response was not, "Cool!" as I expected. There was not one "Thank you." However, one kid said it all, "Nice, I'll be warm tonight." Like I said resource.

They pile out of the *dojo*, filthy socks, dirty necks, and coats that protect them from the cold and the rest of us from their body odor. The world has put tremendous dents into the psyche of these kids. I wish them well and hope that eventually they will take their skills of cleverness and smarts and bring them to bear on the programs that are available to them to get their lives back together.

As I tuned to the mirror, I saw some smears of street-filth on my *gi* as we had rolled a bit. But, they left a little more than that on me, stuff that couldn't be seen in the mirror. I hope I was able to leave a little something for them too.

Making it real...

Many reading this book teach martial arts. For some it's a hobby, for others an occupation. Regardless, we all have valuable knowledge, skills, and abilities to share, things that can make a lasting impact on others. Consider using some of that wealth to give back. Plant a seed in your community. You never know what is going to take root.

CHAPTER THIRTY-SIX

MARTIAL ARTS TRAINING TIP #62

"You are never too old to set another goal or to dream a new dream." – C. S. Lewis

Actually we just made up the #62, but the behavior, the training tip, it is not fictional. This is about flawed thinking, filtering. Filtering is when you take details and magnify them to the extreme, distorting actual events. A single element is picked out and the whole event becomes colored by this facet.

How do you know you're doing it? Filtering is the internal voice that tells you that you will never be good at martial arts because you made a mistake. A great example of this was portrayed on the Chris Farley Show. For those of you who never watched it or don't recall, here's a link to an example: http://www.youtube.com/watch?v=jNBlyGxV7Ek.

The negative thinking of all-or-nothing is an absolute progress killer. One little screw-up and bang, your confidence is in the gutter. All the positives are flushed down the toilet because you can't get past the failure. You will know this behavior by these words rattling around in your head, "Always, Never, Can't, Every Time." All-or-nothing thinking is associated with negative thinking. "Oh, I always do that!" when you make a mistake, or "I suck at this." "I'll never get this right."

Here is a little reveal for you students out there. We instructors know that when you verbalize a comment like, "I'll never get it right" you have said in your mind so many times during your internal dialogue that you are comfortable saying the thought aloud. Saying a thought means that you believe it and, at least subconsciously, want us to believe it as well. When these words are uttered by you, you might notice by our slumped shoulders or hangdog expressions, this is because we know that this thinking is deeply embedded in your psyche. If only we could reach into your head and rip it out... but unfortunately it's not as simple as all that.

But there is a "cure." For those of you that use final, broad, and wildly inclusive words in your negative internal conversation, just stop it. Really; it's just that simple and that challenging, but you can retrain your brain merely by changing your vocabulary. To be successful you must be relentless in driving those words out of your mind. Hunt these words down, stalk them, and kill them immediately. Terminate with no remorse.

So there you have it, Martial Arts Training Tip #62. The title is fake, the contents real.

Making it real...

Do not use words like "Always, Never, Can't, Every Time." Dig them out of your thinking and bury them deep. Replace them with phrases like "This is difficult," "I haven't succeeded yet," "I'll get this right soon enough," or "I'm working on it." You get the idea... With this new mental model problems are transformed into challenges, bumps in the road rather than insurmountable obstacles. Once you start to think that way say it aloud and keep saying it out loud in order to lock it in. It's amazing what a simple change in phraseology can do for your perspective, your outlook on life not just on martial arts.

CHAPTER THIRTY-SEVEN

NOTHING SAYS LOSER LIKE...

"Nothing says loser like, 'I was kicked out of a cult.'"
                                                    – Blind Date

Recently we have had an intermittent flurry of conversations with martial artists regarding instructors and their behavior. These types of conversations always boil down to a few key points:

- My instructor says I am not committed enough to [insert name here] art
- The instructors' definition of commitment is physically or mentally unhealthy
- My choice is to submit to the definition or leave the club
- I don't want to leave, but I don't care to buy into the program as presented

The biggest issue is the sense of guilt that the person feels. The guilt that they have not worked hard enough, that they have lost something, or that they have failed. There's a pile of other emotions too, of course, but guilt overrides.

Let's get this straight. It's *your* training. You're paying for it, investing your time in it, so if you don't enjoy it, if it is causing you some form of consternation, you should stop.

The world is a tough place and it doesn't give a flying rip about how you feel. We get kicked around every day—traffic, bills, work, difficult responsibilities, hard choices, illnesses, etc. We're confident you can add a whole lot more to the list. The point is, are going to go take guff from your martial arts instructor? We don't mean him or her challenging you to be better, that's goodness, but rather poorly constructed coursework, lousy coaching, incompetent instruction, or even cult-like behavior. Yeah go pay for *that* with your hard-earned money and further invest more of your time?! Pffft... We think not.

Just because someone is an outstanding martial arts practitioner doesn't automatically mean they're a decent person... or that they know how to teach effectively. So, we respectfully suggest that if you are not having fun, not learning as you think you should, you should leave. It's not like there are no other instructors out there if the one you've found isn't a good fit for how you learn.

You only live once, so choose wisely how you spend that life. After all, it belongs to you not others. We're talking about the sanctity of the individual—your choices, your destiny. If you're in a dysfunctional relationship with your teacher(s) you're not necessary involved in a cult, but getting kicked out of a martial arts club can make you feel like a loser nonetheless.

Well, let's see what that illustrious philosopher and social scientist Marx had to say about the subject. Of course we mean Groucho Marx, not that other guy... He said, "I don't care to belong to any club that accepts people like me as members."

Making it real...

It takes enthusiasm, hard work, and adherence to the curriculum to achieve at just about anything, yet if devotion turns to fanaticism, respectful deference to blind obedience, you've over-rotated. Here's the middle ground, a declaration you've heard before but that bears repeating, "Karate is fun. When it stops being fun, you should stop doing it." Same goes for any hobby, martial art, volunteer opportunity, or other use of your time. After all, it is *your* time, your life, and your priorities.

CHAPTER THIRTY-EIGHT

THAT'S PROFILING DAD

"The best vision is insight."

– Malcolm Forbes

As we pulled into my parking space that weekday afternoon, I spotted two young men ambling through the alleyway. When I said aloud, "They don't belong here," my son piped up, "That's profiling Dad. That is sooooo wrong!"

The guys in the alley were dressed in jeans and oversize t-shirts, and wore red baseball caps cocked at a 45°... out of place and out of time. They dressed like punks, not full on gangbanger, but wannabe fashion. In the alley, not the sidewalk, to add to the formula, they had no hurry in their step and a plastic bag hung from one of their hands. This might be trouble, nothing to act on, just unusual enough to take note as daytime burglaries had been on the rise throughout the neighborhood recently.

That's what flashed through my head in the few seconds I observed the situation. But then my son yelled out the accusatory and pejorative term "profiling." What I heard was not, "That's profiling Dad..." Right, wrong, or indifferent, what I heard was my son say was, "It is wrong for you to make a threat assessment based on what you observe."

A headshake joined my wide eyes as I began to channel the comedian Louis Black. I launched into a mini lecture on behaviors of the animal kingdom, common sense, how observing a potential threat is not a bad thing, but in fact a very good thing! My diatribe may not have completely washed away the slush of a notion from a society that teaches folks to not use their common sense, but apparently I did make some headway.

Two days later, he said to me, "I saw those two guys again yesterday Dad. It looks like they're working on a house up the block and were just walking back from the minimart when we saw them."

Ah... lesson learned, lesson applied.

Making it real...

Profiling isn't equal. In other words, we can probably all agree that racial profiling is a bad thing, it smacks of racism, yet behavioral profiling is a very good thing—it's how El Al Airlines keeps travelers safe from hijackings, how security forces identify would-be suicide bombers, how the Secret Service spots potential troublemakers, and how civilians concerned with self-defense avoid looming dangers. Oftentimes behavioral profiling, that is identifying patterns of behavior that warrant closer attention, is necessary for assuring your survival. Remove the blinders and observe the world as it is, not as social niceties expect it to be.

CHAPTER THIRTY-NINE

HELPING KARATEKA ACHIEVE THEIR GOALS

"It is good to have an end to journey toward; but it is the journey that matters in the end."

– Ernest Hemmingway

Okay the quote above sounds all nice, fuzzy, and easy to say. For somebody who teaches martial arts, however, it is not as easy as just showing up and gently shoving in the general direction of somebody's expressed goal. That is not a recipe for success over the long run. Success, in this instance, is defined as a long and enjoyable run where training in the martial arts is and remains beneficial for the student.

Aiding somebody in reaching their goals is a wild mix of the students' needs, wants, and desires, plus your agenda as a teacher. Now let's complicate it further by making it a moving target. Did your goals change as you progressed through the ranks? Did you as a person morph, change, and grow during the pursuit of your martial arts goals? The answer, of course, is yes.

The question then becomes, who is responsible for that transformation? Are you, the teacher responsible for the transformation? Is it other people in the school? The student him/herself? Or, is it a combination?

Helping others reach their goals is not a static target and yet we would hope that our discipline as a teacher will provide the laser-like focus on the target that is necessary to reach the goal. That's flawed thinking. You see, the target is not a target, but a path. While students still see it as a target, those of us who teach can have a broader perspective.

For students, know this: You will start with a target, but you and the target are going to change along the way. Your goal will eventually become a path if you train in the martial arts long enough.

Getting all Philosophy 101 here, for students the target forms the path. Oftentimes you don't know you are on the path for focusing on the target. Instructors have had targets too, but are now on a path. So, helping somebody reach their goal is a lot more complicated than just putting them through the paces. Targets move, appear and disappear. Agendas change. When a good path rises, it should be chosen.

Making it real...

Have you noticed that ranks in the martial arts form a pyramid? For all the thousands who have trained at one time or another, practically everyone you meet took judo or taekwondo or something "as a kid," only a handful earn their black belt (or equivalent rank). Fewer still progress through advanced ranks toward further promotion. Oftentimes they either meet their initial goal and then drop out or lose interest along the way. Do you have a place, a time in your martial journey that you can point to where the target fell away and the path appeared? How did you recognize it? It's not enlightenment, at least not in the traditional definition of the term, yet being able to point to that place in time is one way of helping others see the larger world that martial arts can become. Perhaps in this fashion we can blunt that pyramid, making it something more akin to a square, where less folks drop out as they rise through the ranks.

CHAPTER FORTY

SOCRATES, RORY MILLER, AND EARTHWORMS

"Life is really simple, but we insist on making it complicated."

– Confucius

Our conversations with Rory Miller often leave us with points to ponder. He's one of those guys who sees the world a little differently, takes things in a little more deeply than other people do. And, he gets those around him to think deeper thoughts than they normally tend to do. During one conversation, Kris was lamenting on the issue of the moment and Rory responded with something that set the wheels churning in Kris's head.

Rory said, "Kris, life is easy. I see stupid people do it all the time."

See, simple yet profound. After a little pondering, Kris realized that Rory was right. An earthworm is not smart, but it does do life pretty darn well. Sure it is a simple life, but it does it easily. So yeah, not that complicated, not that hard. Bore holes in the earth, eat, and reproduce.

Being creative, in our opinion is one of those vital things that changes life from being just an existence into something greater. Creativity leads you to examine your life. Some folks paint, sculpt, build things from wood or metal, or use some other external medium as their vehicle of expression. Martial artists, on the other hand, find expression through their bodies and minds. It is upon this metaphorical canvas, that we express ourselves, hence are transformed in a deliberate and creative manner.

Being a martial artist makes you examine your life and, well, in the immortal words of Socrates, "An unexamined life is not worth living."

After throwing Rory Miller and Socrates into the blender along with fresh squeezed lime and a little ice and you get a potent cocktail, one we express as:

"Martial arts help you to examine your life, to do more than just exist."

Making it real...

When did you realize that your art had changed you? Through rigorous training some of us find the strength to walk away from confrontations, the discipline to achieve laudable goals, or the vitality to pursue our dreams. In what ways has the examination of your life through martial arts made a positive difference? How can you pay it forward and pass that on?

CHAPTER FORTY-ONE

SMITH'S RULES
OF DESIGN, #3

"Manifest plainness, embrace simplicity, reduce selfishness, and have few desires."

– Lao Tzu

In the August 2008 issue of *Popular Mechanics* magazine is a great article titled, "Smith's Rules of Design." In this chapter we'll discuss Rule #3: "Do the hard work needed to find a simple solution."

As Leonardo da Vinci once said, "Simplicity is the ultimate sophistication." This the key to lasting designs. Nature builds complexity out of simple commands. Flowers, bugs and you, all made up of simple elements, repetitive, simple commands. The biggest rock in the world is in Australia. Uluru, also referred to as Ayers Rock, has outlasted everything man has ever built and likely will ever build. Simple, elegant, exactly what it is supposed to be—the world's biggest rock.

The old saying goes, "Dumb as a rock." However, when it comes to the simplicity of being what it is supposed to be (built out of simple commands) Uluru has us all beat. To put it in today's vernacular, K.I.S.S., no, not the rock band, the admonition, "Keep It Simple, Stupid."

It is important that your martial arts reflect this understanding. In our world, simplicity truly is the ultimate sophistication.

Making it real...

We've already talked about martial arts practice, so this time we'll address training. Those of us who were trained in the old ways, heck most of us who train at all; we've all seen how challenging our instructors explanations can be. Oftentimes this is a result of our tendency to categorize everything, every nuance, and give it a name. For example, most every art uses throws, sweeps, and takedowns. We can force our students to memorize a whole bunch of techniques, or we can help them learn a few simple principles and improvise. *Osoto gari* sweeps the entire length of the opponent's leg, whereas *osoto gake* chops at his ankle. The difference is cosmetic; you're simply removing the opponent's source of balance and stability, the one he or she is most reliant on. The end result, either way, opponent falls down goes boom... So, while it's nice to be able to name a bazillion different sweeps, why not focus primarily on the fundamental principles that make them work effectively. Students learn faster, perform better, and ultimately stick around far, far longer when we make things easy for them to understand.

CHAPTER FORTY-TWO

DIRT UNDER YOUR FINGERNAILS

"I'm a dirt person. I trust the dirt. I don't trust diamonds and gold."

– Eartha Kitt

Kris had a professor in college who announced one day that, "You should never trust a man with perfect fingernails." With that statement, Kris became an instant fan of that guy's classes of which he took three. You see, Kris's background was from a farm, an agricultural community, one that was so dependent on farming that they closed school for two weeks every fall so that the kids could help their parents bring in the harvest.

When a kid took school off for the harvest break but didn't work, that placed him or her in a different category. These kids were seen as people who didn't know how to work. What that professor validated was, don't trust anybody who doesn't do whatever they're trying to teach. The implication is that they don't understand.

This applies to far more than manual labor. For those of you that have one or more college degrees and are using them today, when did you learn the most about what you do for a living? Studies suggest that 70% of learning is experiential. Did you learn more in the classroom or the first year or two out in the field plying your skills on the job?

It has been stated many times before, differently, and perhaps even better, but we like this analogy: When it comes to the martial arts don't have perfect finger nails. Get dirty, get slivers; get them smashed, and bashed, and mangled.

Go out and get some dirt under your fingernails.

Making it real...

Attending a lecture, reading a book, watching a DVD or YouTube video, these are all great means of broadening your horizons. But, they are no substitute for spending time on the *dojo* floor practicing what you've read, heard, and seen. If you truly want to progress in your art, get your fingernails dirty. *Rondori* (free sparring) in judo, for example, lets you feel the contact, the movement, the balance, position, and timing, all vital elements of applying technique successfully.

CHAPTER FORTY-THREE

THE CONCLUSION COMES WITH CLARITY

"Pain is a relatively objective, physical phenomenon; suffering is our psychological resistance to what happens. Events may create physical pain, but they do not in themselves create suffering. Resistance creates suffering. Stress happens when your mind resists what is... The only problem in your life is your mind's resistance to life as it unfolds."

– Dan Millman

Miyamoto Musashi (1584–1645) was born Shinmen Takezō. He grew up in the Harima Province of Japan. Arguably, the greatest swordsman who ever lived, Musashi slew his first opponent, Arima Kihei, at the age of 13. Considered *Kensei*, the sword saint of Japan, Musashi killed more than sixty trained samurai warriors in fights or duals during the feudal period where even a minor battle injury could lead to infection and death. He was the founder of the *Hyōhō Niten Ichi-Ryu* style of swordsmanship, which translates as "two heavens as one" or "two-sword style." Like most samurai, he was skilled in the peaceful arts as well, an exceptional poet, calligrapher, and artist. Two years before he died, Musashi retired to a life of seclusion in a cave where he codified his winning strategy in the famous *Go Rin No Sho* which, in English, translates as *The Book of Five Rings*.

If you search through *The Book of Five Rings* you will find the admonition that a person should be familiar with all martial arts (he was specifically referring to the various sword schools found in feudal Japan at the time). Musashi also goes on to make the distinction between being familiar with versus fully understanding other arts. He does not suggest mastering every art, just knowing enough about them to strategically use that knowledge against your adversary in a fight.

Between the two of us, we have spent time with *Goju Ryu* karate, *Shotokan* karate, Taekwondo, *Hung-gar*, *Arnis*, Judo, Aikido, *Kendo*, Brazilian Jujitsu, *Kenpo*, Tai Chi, *Iaido*, and *Matayoshi Kobudo*, not to mention boxing, wrestling, shooting sports, and modern close-quarters combatives. You know what this experience has given us beyond a somewhat more than average appraisal of what's out there? Certainty—a conviction that what we are training now is what's right for us. This conclusion comes with clarity because we have had, and still have, the intellectual curiosity to explore other arts. A curiosity fostered by our parents, teachers, and various martial arts instructors.

Now obviously we cannot master, nor could we try every art that is out there. That is impossible. Nevertheless, a sampling allows us to become "familiar" as Musashi puts it. We liken it to a child who is resistant to trying a new food. They do not want to try it because they are confident that they know what it tastes like and in a fit of immaturity turn up their nose to something that they have never experienced.

Some of our students have gone off to other arts, leaving our school permanently. Other students have returned after knocking around the martial arts world a bit. Other students have found some other pursuit that lights them up more than martial arts and no longer train.

Our response to all of these paths is, "cool."

Making it real...

Get out there and explore. There are more diverse opportunities in the martial arts available nowadays than we have ever known in the history of mankind. Get out there and try something new; you do not have to marry it, you can just date it for a while. It's not only okay to knock around a bit, it's a very good idea; one that leads to certainty when you find your place in the martial arts world.

CHAPTER FORTY-FOUR

NOT ME, NOT HERE!

"Do you want to know who you are? Don't ask. Act! Action will delineate and define you."

– Thomas Jefferson

Having taught woman's self-defense classes now and again over the last twenty five or more years, we have tried to convey that there is no magic technique for success. In fact, no matter what your gender, when an attacker chooses you as his (or her) prey they are confident they can get what they want. Bad guys don't want a fair fight, they want to win.

Not that long ago a 55-year-old woman in the Seattle area was viciously beaten by a potential rapist who assaulted her during her evening run. He knocked her down, brandished a knife, broke her nose, and fractured her face. Nevertheless, this indomitable woman refused to be a victim and fought back. She did not use any special tactics that she learned in a woman's self-defense class. There was no well-placed eye gouge or kick to the balls. She used her will to not be raped, to not die. In fact she yelled out, "Not me, not here!" and fought back with little skill, but every ounce of ferocity she could muster.

Clearly there are a lot of factors that these incidents bring up, but our point here is that her desire, her guts, are what trumped any defensive tactics class she could have taken. It's not the technique, but the attitude, the size of the fight in the dog, rather than the size of the dog in the fight as it were... And attitude is damnably hard to train in any self-defense seminar; there's simply not enough time to reach anyone that deeply.

If we were to talk to her, what we'd say to this gutsy, gutsy woman is, "Well done!"

Well done on fighting off a determined predator. Well done in getting an extensive description of the guy and providing it to the police. Thank you for the example. Thank you for showing that the will, the will to fight, to declare "Not me, not here!" is the deepest rooted part of any self-defense. And, we wish a swift and complete recovery for you, one that comes with lots of support from family and friends.

Whether you realize it or not you're a hero.

If you are interested in learning more about the aforementioned attack here's a link to the *Seattle*

Times article: http://seattletimes.nwsource.com/html/
localnews/2013154472_attack14m.html.

Making it real...

"Will drills," activities that test your limits and help you learn to fight to a defined goal are an important aspect of holistic self-defense training. One example you may have heard of is the 30-man *kumite* (which you can read about in Goran Powell's book *Waking Dragons*). But, such activities don't necessarily even have to relate directly to martial arts in order to add value. Consider, for example, *Outward Bound* and similar outdoor adventure programs that can help you test yourself in a controlled but extraordinarily challenging environment. Whatever the method you choose, push yourself, test your limits, and help build the will survive that can help you prevail in a violent encounter.

CHAPTER FORTY-FIVE

KARATE PURITANS

"The reason I talk to myself is because I'm the only one whose answers I accept."

– George Carlin

About every other month, Kris gets a phone call or an e-mail from a certain type of prospective student. These folks are what he calls the "Karate Puritans." The Puritans, for those unfamiliar, came from England to America (circa the 16th and 17th centuries). They advocated more "purity of worship" as doctrine, hence the name.

When these Karate Puritans make contact, they start with a menu of, "Do you...?" You can append that with anything you would like at this point, because the testing has begun. After an indeterminate period of questioning they will find an issue of divergence, a possible deal-breaker to their purity test.

By this point, it is clear that the person calling or e-mailing is seeking something: A re-creation of what he or she once had, or maybe the purity of the "one true way."

You get the point... The *dojo* has to be just so and the instruction should be exactly the way they have envisioned. At the end of the day, the Karate Puritans, while their cup is not empty it is not full of technique or experience either. Instead, their cup is full of expectations, goals, and preconceptions of what should be and that leaves little if any room for anything else.

In our experience more often than not these Karate Puritans use the pattern of questioning to not train, to not get on the floor, to not apply themselves. In searching for perfection they suffer from analysis paralysis. Always analyzing, never doing.

Now some of the Karate Puritans have shown up at the *dojo*. Sometimes they just watch, other times they train for awhile, but none of them stay for any significant amount of time. In fact, we cannot remember one ever staying and training for more than a few weeks. It is because they are busy finding a reason not to stay.

At the end of the day, in our world, that's just fine.

Making it real...

Perhaps having dabbled in a plethora of styles we're more open-minded than most, but it seems to us that the instructor is far more important than the art. After all, a martial arts experience can and should be far more than punching, kicking, throwing, and such. Once you find the right instructor, the right environment in which to train, that's a thing of value, one we'd assert is far greater than puritanical adherence to any specific style. Characteristics of an exemplary instructor include enthusiasm for his/her art, a passion for teaching, a well-rounded knowledge of *budo* (martial arts), a high degree of perception regarding the needs and interests of students, the ability to communicate a sense of direction and purpose for his/her school, and an open-mind, tempered with a great deal of common sense. And, the ideal teacher must also have a high degree of integrity, personal honor, and strong moral character. Be puritanical about finding the "right" instructor, but stay open-minded when it comes to the martial style that person teaches.

CHAPTER FORTY-SIX

SMITH'S RULES
OF DESIGN, #7

"Give a man a fish and you feed him for a day. Teach a man to fish and you feed him for a lifetime."

– Chinese Proverb

In the August 2008 issue of *Popular Mechanics* magazine is a great article titled, "Smith's Rules of Design." In this chapter we'll discuss Rule #7: "Provide skills, not just finished technologies."

The current revolution in design for developing countries is the notion of co-creation, of teaching the skills necessary to create the solution, rather than simply providing the solution. By involving the community throughout the design process, you can help equip people to contribute—they acquire the skills needed to create solutions to a much wider variety of problems. In other words, transferring technology is good, but transferring the skill to improve the technology is better.

If you are an instructor you have the responsibility to transfer the skill of improving technique to your students. If you are not, you are remiss in your duties. You know the Chinese Proverb, "Give a man a fish..." Well, this is the same. As a teacher you must have the desire and the vision to teach your students about discernment and exploration.

By discernment, we mean the ability of the student to understand what is going on and to use good judgment in applying what they've learned. Exploration is defined in terms of seeking the next horizon, looking past the immediate to understand consequences and implications, to gather more.

These two concepts make a potent combination. Instilling these skills means that your students can venture and learn anywhere. And, more importantly they will know the difference between the good and the garbage. This builds value that lasts far beyond whatever time the pupil is in your charge, something he or she can leverage for a lifetime.

Making it real...

Early in training, say at the white and yellow belt levels of most systems, concepts need to be dosed out in small increments to avoid overwhelming students. However, once those early fundamentals have been mastered it is incumbent upon instructors to provide more. Stop spoon-feeding and use a fire hose. Not everything will be absorbed, but as students become ready for more and more knowledge important details will sort themselves out in their minds. Mastery of martial arts is far, far more than passing a multiple choice test. It's holistically understanding and applying what has been taught, making it your own, and adding more. Our goal as instructors should be to provide the framework and understanding that allows students to get there whenever they are ready.

CHAPTER FORTY-SEVEN

I QUIT DRINKING MY COFFEE

"I have learned over the years that when one's mind is made up, this diminishes fear. Knowing what must be done does away with fear."

– Rosa Parks

I quit drinking my coffee; I just sat silently, listening to each part of the story as it unfolded. She and her husband had been subjected to a home-invasion robbery. Someone knocked on the door of their duplex. Once they opened it to see who was there, two men burst in, one holding a gun. The homeowners, one a priest and the other an attorney, found themselves looking down the barrel of a gun as one of the robbers shouted, "Give us the drugs!" while the other began ransacking the apartment.

More questions followed—something about a baby. Yes, apparently the drug dealers these guys were seeking had a baby. And, the names didn't match. The criminals figured it out fairly quickly... they had the wrong duplex. They meant to have robbed the place next door.

This is where the story really gave me chills... "They taped us up in our chairs so they could rob the duplex next door," she said.

This scenario illustrates one of my personal "non-negotiables." Consequently as she went on with the telling, I found it hard to listen because of the adrenaline rush buzzing in my head.

I decided long ago that faced with a similar situation, I would never allow myself to be tied up. I was never going to allow myself to be transported to a secondary crime scene either. Knowing what that often means, I have vowed to fight with all I have to keep these two things from happening. More often than not, being tied up and/or transported ends badly, usually with notification of your next of kin when the authorities eventually find your mutilated body.

It turned out, of course, that she was successful in her strategy of compliance. Getting to know the attackers, helping them realize that she was an individual, a person—it worked. After all, she was here to tell me about it. But, she beat the odds with that outcome. Statistically it shouldn't have worked out that way. Obviously I'm thrilled that it did, very pleased by the positive conclusion as she's a wonderful lady and I'd never want to see her hurt.

After talking with her more, I believe, and clearly this only one man's opinion, that the usual scenario was never the assailants' intent. Here's why: The gunman stood close to her *and* he talked. The gun is a weapon of distance. Demanding no communication with the victim allows for objectification, which makes it psychologically easier to use that distance weapon to kill.

That was not the pattern here, so it appears they had no intent to kill anybody, only threaten. Now this event could have gone in any direction really fast, and there is a lot of information to plumb through, but my point is that my prior decision-making had kicked in (the adrenalin surge) even sitting over a cup of coffee and listening to an event that happened to somebody else.

Making it real...

Do you have a policy or two, actions you would take if such an event happened to you? What about an earthquake or flood, or even a car accident? Think about it now when things are calm, when you have time and safety to make a plan. How far are you willing to go? What are you prepared to do, or not do, what are you willing to have done to you when faced with a dire threat? A little preparation can go a long way.

CHAPTER FORTY-EIGHT

THE INTERNETS

"Patience and perseverance have a magical effect before which difficulties disappear and obstacles vanish."

– John Quincy Adams

When we grew up ordering a record album could take all day. At best it meant a drive to the record store, at worst it meant driving all around town or wading through the phonebook calling place after place until we found the one that had what we were looking for in stock. Nowadays, you can download just about anything from the internet in a few seconds.

Recently a parent asked, "How much longer until my kid gets a black belt?" Notice she didn't say, "Earns a black belt."

These two instances, ordering music on the internet and the parent seeking a timeline, are very different and yet much the same. The commonality is immediacy. A generation ago asking after a timeline for black belt would have been unthinkable. Well, to be honest, in youthful ignorance and impatience we both asked... once..., but, oooohh neither of us ever did *that* again. It simply was not done.

But today, today we have to handle those sorts of "When is my next test?" questions differently than our instructors did. The reason is that we live in a short-attention-span theater generation, one where most people buy songs, books, clothes, and even groceries off the web. They use a "fast pass" to pay the tolls on the highway, not even stopping or slowing down, just whizzing by. Heck, nobody waits in line for concert tickets anymore either; they simply pay with a credit card and download them onto a smart phone or other device.

So, in a world where many if not most needs and desires are met almost instantly, why would the martial arts be any different?

The difference is this. To buy a really good musical instrument, say a guitar, you go shopping at a brick-and-mortar store, one with actual salespeople who know something about their products. You need to see the guitar in person, feel it, and play it a bit. You might do some research on the web, of course, most folks do, but the purchase of an expensive musical instrument takes time and actual physical contact.

That's something you just can't get on the internet. You have to spend time and feel the art, meld with the instrument. You need to meld yourself with the techniques of your art too. The one thing that cannot be compressed, downloaded, or e-mailed is time spent on the *dojo* floor.

Making it real...

Are you a victim of fast food culture? Do you really, really want it now, need it instantly, and can't wait no matter what? Probably not; chances are you wouldn't be reading this book if you fall into that category. But, chances are equally good if not better that your students and/or those in your sphere of influence might have a bad case of the "gotta have it nows." Help them see the larger picture. Some things truly are worth waiting for. After all, more often than not the tougher a thing is to earn the more it's appreciated.

CHAPTER FORTY-NINE

TEENAGE GIRL
GETS A BEAT-DOWN

"The main goal of the future is to stop violence. The world is addicted to it."

– Bill Cosby

You might have read the story, it made national news: A teenage girl gets beat down savagely in a Metro Bus tunnel by another teen. And it all happens in front of contracted, uniformed security personnel. For the next couple weeks everybody is pulling their hair out over this. All the radio talk shows are going off, some calling out the manliness of the guards, companies defending their security policy, governments calling for reviews, and politicians getting outraged.

Everybody is in a dust up, screaming that something should have, could have, and would have been done differently. But not us... We're going to blow right past all this folderol and simply say, "Violence happens." There are bad people out there, intent on doing you harm. There always have been and always will be. Not just bullies, but real life honest-to-badness predators too. Let's face it, this girl who kicked the other girl in the head... she's one of the bad people.

Good people and bad people aside, it seems like this sort of thing is happening more and more often lately. After all, YouTube is chock full of public beat downs captured on video, right? Are we just hearing more about events like this, or is something shifting in society? In other words, what is the crux of this event?

Well... what would you honestly expect from a society that teaches compliance? From an early age, children are taught to not take matters into their own hands, to instead seek out an authority figure who has the right and the power to make things right. Further, as a kid we are all taught that the defender often gets the same punishment as the offender. For example, a common policy in US schools today is that both kids get expelled for fighting, no matter who started it. So, in the bus tunnel incident you have security guards who had been taught that there is no reward for intervention, only punishment. And, their company's policies support that belief.

Now, before you go off and suggest that we believe fighting resolves all issues, don't go there. Our track-record is pretty clear. What we are saying, is that as a human being you have a right to defend yourself and a responsibility to act, when necessary, to implement that right. By outsourcing your individual responsibility to some other authority, the school, the government, whatever, you're conditioning yourself to become a victim.

The more you pull on this thread the more aspects of this event unravel, but we want to stick to this narrow point. We now have:

- A stratum of society, the law abiding "good" people, who follow the rules that have been established for reasonable and safe interactions amongst individuals

- A second stratum of society, the "bad" people, who intuitively understand that all those other guys are an easy resource to take advantage of

These bad people know that the others will seek authority and that takes time. Further, they also know that, like the impotent security guards in the bus tunnel, authority is often a paper tiger.

How's this bus tunnel incident going to end? After review, the policies will be found to be in order yet they will be tweaked a little to make everyone feel better. The guards will keep their jobs because they followed their company's polices (and if terminated will have grounds for a lawsuit).

The girl who got beaten down will have a long and painful recovery punctuated with a giant pile of medical bills. The bad girl who kicked the bejesus out of the other one will wind up in court, get a slap on the wrist, and in all likelihood be placed on some form of parole. Assuming she's a juvenile, her record will be wiped clean upon reaching her majority.

And, the rest of the people will avoid that bus tunnel for a little while because bad things happened there. Will society learn any lessons from all this? We think it's a safe bet that it will not.

Society may not learn... but perhaps a select few of us will. We'll think about our personal safety a little differently. Think, and act.

Hubert Humphrey once wrote, "There are not enough jails, not enough policemen, not even enough courts to enforce a law not supported by the people." We'd take that a step farther and say, "There are not enough jails, policemen, or courts to protect people who are unwilling to look out for themselves."

Making it real...

Be responsible and accountable for your own safety. You're a martial artist so chances are reasonable that you know a thing or two about fighting, but have you studied the situations and circumstances under which you might have to employ those skills for self-protection? Do you know the applicable laws; understand where, when, and how you can apply countervailing force. And, do you know how to articulate the need to physically defend yourself in ways that won't cook your own goose before a judge or jury? Self defense is much, much more than fighting.

CHAPTER FIFTY

ONE WHO REFLECTS UPON

"Truth is confirmed by inspection and delay; falsehood by haste and uncertainty."

– Tacitus

Recently a museum in the state of Ohio was disappointed to discover that the lock of Amelia Earhart's hair they sent to a DNA lab turned out not to belong to the famous pilot. In fact, it wasn't even a lock of hair at all, but rather a piece thread. The news was embarrassing for the institution, clearly. After all, museum curators are supposed to be experts in their fields.

The moral of this story is that you should question, and question a lot—especially when it comes to the martial arts, boxing, wrestling, or what have you. Now we are not talking about militant rejections and the assumption that everything you run into might be false, just metered, healthy skepticism.

By skepticism we mean in the terms of its original use of the word; rooted in the Greek "*skeptikos*," which translates as, "One who reflects upon something."

Many folks reflect on the micro aspects of their training. What is this movement for? How is it applied? We submit, however, that you should also be reflecting upon the purpose of your training. Every so often we'll ask students in the beginning adults class why they're training. Responses are always enlightening. We hear things like, "To get tougher," "To learn an art", "To protect myself," and "To get exercise and learn something useful too."

And a few people stammer, lacking a coherent answer. They are the ones who haven't really thought too much about what they were doing or why. They just feel the draw to come to a *dojo* and lay down their hard-earned money to attend class.

As with the museum, where curators assumed they had a lock of Amelia Earhart's hair, yet discovered they had been confused by a piece of thread, you are making assumptions about your martial arts. Have you really sat down and reflected on the reason why you are doing what you are doing?

We did. After a long internal conversation Kris, for example, began to pare it down, to chip away at the words, reducing the paragraph to a couple of sentences and then reducing it even more. Finally he got it down to one word. And that was it, the reason that he trains.

Making it real...

Take the time and reflect on your art. Relax, take time, but be brutal in your self-auditing until you get to the core. You need to know if you are looking at a thread or a hair.

CHAPTER FIFTY-ONE

POETRY AND TEACHING

"Poetry is when you make new things familiar and familiar things new." – Rory Sutherland

The quote above comes from adman Rory Sutherland, and was used in his TED lecture. TED is a nonprofit agency devoted to spreading ideas, usually in the form of short, powerful talks that last 18 minutes or less. Created in 1984 as a conference where Technology, Entertainment, and Design converged, hence the acronym TED, today the organization covers topics ranging from science to business to global issues in more than 100 languages around the world.

Sutherland's TED presentation was about the elevation of experience and what we value in life, yet it directly applies to martial arts. We find that quote a crystallization of what we try to do. After years of being on the floor training and teaching martial arts, this guy just brought it all together.

We strive to make classes accessible by using stories and analogies. For example *Sensei* Jeff Stevens, another instructor at West Seattle Karate Academy, is known for saying, "If you need to peel potatoes, you peel potatoes here," and he pulls his hands inward, "Not out here," as he extends his hands. His point is that you may or may not recognize the concept of keeping your arms in, but odds are good that you do know peeling potatoes. Or carrots. He takes new information and makes it familiar.

The other end of that concept, making the familiar new, that is really for the black belts. How do you drive them deeper into their own research? How do you make the familiar new? One way we do it is what we call the breakdown. We take a small section of the art that we can dissect, examine, train it, and then bring it back into the totality of the art.

So yeah, to get all hoitie toitie for a second, we try and make each of our classes a form of poetry, all William Shakespeare n' stuff. And you should too.

Making it real...

It's a metaphor and a challenge... to get more from your martial art figure out where you can find the poetry in what you do. How do you make new things familiar, familiar things new? People experience the world through their senses, sight, sound, smell, and touch. For better learning, and a richer *dojo* experience, reach out to as many of the senses as possible. Tell stories, explain things so that folks can hear... and understand. Demonstrate so they can see... and emulate. Practice so they can feel... and do.

CHAPTER FIFTY-TWO

THEY HID IT,
BUT NOT IN THE FORM

"Education is the movement from darkness to light."
— Allan Bloom

We believe in the commonly held notion that the martial artists of yesteryear hid their art. It wasn't just post-World War II Okinawa where instructors made their living teaching to occupying GIs, hence not only had a language barrier to overcome but were also reticent to share overmuch with former enemies, martial arts teachers throughout history have always been careful about who they taught things to. They hid their arts from others so that they would have an advantage over any potential attacker. Common sense stuff, right?

The American military has, on occasion, blown up its own downed aircraft. They make sure the pilots are clear of the wreckage, lock in onto the plane, swoop down and, boom... Disintegrated! This ensures that cutting-edge technology doesn't fall into the enemies' hands. The technology is the edge that makes the difference. In the same way that superior techniques gave an edge to the ancient masters, a technological edge in modern battle means we win, you lose.

So yeah, they hid stuff. However, not like a lot of people think. The American military does not hide how to use the aircraft from its pilots. We are confident that this conversation between the engineers and the instructors has never taken place, "Hey Chet, let's make this stealth fighter hard to fly and then hide some of the skills needed to fly it from the pilot! No, no, no, wait, wait, aaaaannd we'll teach some of the skills backward, yeah! That's it. Brilliant! Done and done."

It makes no sense at all. So if we take this real-world example to the world of *kata* (forms), it makes no sense to hide, obfuscate, or try to bury a technique to be discovered only after years of hard study either. Back in the ancient master's day people didn't have as much free time. Time devoted to martial arts was the purview of the military, the rich, and those few dedicated people who fell into the remaining categories of society.

And, let's face it, they didn't live as long back then as folks tend to do today. Short lives with not much free time meant that practitioners needed to be able to apply what they learned quickly. Without the benefit of modern medicine or law enforcement, they almost assuredly wanted to be able to apply their self-defense skills as fast as possible too. And, likely, to do it well, hiding their skill from the bad guys until they needed to show it.

Taking time away from tending crops, making food, building shelter, or other necessities and spending that precious time on a mind game; that doesn't make a whole lot of sense. So hiding from the bad guys? Yes absolutely. Hiding from the end user? No, not at all.

Making it real...

Instructors: How are you teaching? Are you holding things back? If so, why? If it's teaching fundamentals in building blocks, adding more and more as students' are capable of understanding that's laudable... assuming you have also shown the bigger picture too so that folks can comprehend where they're heading. However, if you're holding back simply because that's the way you were taught; think hard on your motivation. Students: It's your precious time, your money that pays for lessons. Are you getting everything you're paying for?

CHAPTER FIFTY-THREE

OBSESSION IN THE PURSUIT

"An obsession is where something will not leave your mind."

– Eric Clapton

Years ago Lawrence was an apprentice blade-maker for a couple years. Learning to craft knives and swords he spent a fair amount of time around folks who forged steel for a living. Watching a good blacksmith work is fascinating. You can see the obsession: Fever, a deep desire; not only discipline but great skill... and art.

It's intriguing, art is, and it is not hard to find art in the martial arts, art at all levels. When we go to tournaments and judge or watch *kata* we often are not looking for perfection, we are looking for understanding of the form and then an expression of that understanding put to motion.

What happens before the understanding and the expression? It is what comes from the desire, the discipline, and then the explosion of creativity, personalization and... well, beauty. It is the discipline that borders on obsession.

In watching the documentary *It Might Get Loud* you can listen to Jimmy Page of *Led Zeppelin*, Jack White of *The White Stripes*, and The Edge from *U2* talk about the formation of their art. It's fascinating stuff. Jack White took his bed out of his room to make space for musical equipment. Jimmy Page left a well-paying studio job because it stifled his creativity to the point of deep frustration. The Edge realized that it was about the attitude and the emotion for him. Jack White challenges himself today by having instruments a little out of place on stage, just a step too far from where they ought to be, just add a sense of urgency. All three of these men pushed themselves into the unknown in pursuit of their art.

We have stated many times that *kata* is the core of the classical martial arts. *Kata* should be approached as art on one level and the pursuit of the *kata* should, in our opinion, have all of the elements that we touched on: Fever, desire, even obsession. The pursuit of *kata* should involve the desire to achieve more than skill, the desire to become art.

The word obsession, it teeters on imbalance. Hmm... teetering on the edge of imbalance—that's where the action is in pursuit of art.

Making it real...

Few folks want to be average. The average martial artist, he or she goes to class, takes in instruction, works hard, and then goes home. Nothing more. The exceptional martial artist, on the other hand, he or she lives the art, thinks about it constantly, searches, researches, practices and more... And, it's obvious to others in the *dojo*—who's just filling time with taking a class and who's striving for something more. What do you aspire in your pursuit of the art?

CHAPTER FIFTY-FOUR

SMITH'S RULES OF DESIGN, #2

"Success in warfare is gained by carefully accommodating ourselves to the enemy's purpose."

– Sun Tzu

In the August 2008 issue of *Popular Mechanics* magazine is a great article titled, "Smith's Rules of Design." In this chapter we'll discuss Rule #2: "Listen to the right people."

You probably don't know what it's like to carry fifty pounds of firewood on your head. If you're trying to solve a problem related to schlepping around firewood, don't pretend that understand it until you have spoken in-depth with someone who has done it. The key to innovation is in truly understanding the problem, using your imagination is not good enough.

In other words, before you try to solve anything study the problem. It's shocking how many highly paid, highly educated consultants Lawrence has turned away because they came to him with a solution looking for a problem. That's really nothing more than a sales pitch, and an ineffective one at that since they had not studied Lawrence's organization's needs, their value proposition:

> "I can save you $55 million a year by offshoring your service desk to India."

> "Really?! That's amazing since we don't spend anywhere near $55 million a year on our service desk. And, since agents have access to export-controlled information we'd be violating federal ITAR/EAR laws. Somehow saving a couple bucks on a help desk call doesn't seem like a good tradeoff for being debarred as a contractor, losing several billion dollars in business, and spending time in federal prison!"

The Scientific Method is a very effective way of studying a problem, knowing when you've found an effective solution. It works like this:

1) Define the question
2) Gather information and resources (observe)
3) Form hypothesis
4) Perform experiment and collect data
5) Analyze data
6) Interpret data and draw conclusions that serve as a starting point for a new hypothesis

The Scientific Method has gotten the modern world very far. It is the standard of research, the "mother" of invention—good stuff, imperial evidence, and reductive thinking. Likewise, if you use these six points in trying to discern your art, you will go very far.

Science is great, but it is also not enough. The greatest martial artists we have seen have been, as the title implies, artists. They have, or have had, the ability to take a situation and intuit or sense, the situation without much reasoning. They have, through hours of practice, studied the problem. At some point in their mastery they have blended the scientific with the art, hence solved the problem.

Making it real...

How do you study the problem? Let's pretend for a moment that you are a ranked tournament competitor. That means you're strong, fast, and have won again and again in the ring. Does that mean you're prepared to bring those same skills to the street should you need to defend yourself? Likely not... at least not if you haven't studied the problem. For example, in the ring you compete by weight class, winning by submission, knockout, decision, disqualification, or forfeiture. On the street chances are good that you'll be outmatched in size or numbers, there are few if any rules, and you "win" by surviving. That's a profound a difference. Can your skills bridge the gap? Sure. Will they? That's something yet to be determined... Now, increase your odds, go study the problem.

CHAPTER FIFTY-FIVE

I HIRED A JUDOKA

"Toughness is in the soul and spirit, not in muscles."

– Alex Karras

I hired a judoka. Yup, I did. Years ago I had a business that was expanding into the next city and needed somebody to run the store. My business partner and I had talked about some of our options: Placing an ad, looking for a referral, that kind of thing. Unfortunately none of those "usual suspects" had worked horribly well for us in the past. So, I thought about what we were really looking for. We needed quality, dedication, and a "can-do" attitude. And, we also needed somebody who could deal with a potentially contentious public, somebody who could hold their own in any situation.

I remembered this guy, Byron, a judoka. He wasn't in my division, so had I never fought him, but because his matches were always earlier in the day than mine and I had watched him fight on several occasions. I called another judo friend, Bob, and began to describe Byron to him as I didn't actually know Byron's name at the time but figured that Bob who coached extensively would most likely know him. Bob did, and through him I was able to get in contact with Byron.

Turns out, Byron was not only looking for work but was also interested in the position. After an interview, we hired him. The point of the story is that he turned out to be everything we had hoped he would be, not to mention the fact that he had a great sense of humor too.

Even before I knew his name, Byron's martial arts showed his character on the mat. He never displayed a victory dance; he always bowed and followed expected etiquette, and got along well with others in his division. People liked him and respected him as a judo competitor and those things invariably translated directly into the "real world" as well. In a nutshell, the job was his to lose before he ever opened his mouth in the interview.

Making it real...

Those of us who practice martial arts are often reticent to tell others about it. Perhaps we're worried what others might think or say, or perhaps we simply don't realize how well the skills, discipline, and accomplishment of moving through the ranks translate into everyday life. In some ways it's the same as soldiers who wish to move into the civilian world yet struggle to translate their skills despite the fact that leadership under extreme conditions, by way of example, is exactly what's required on many jobs. Whether you're an employer or employee, consider the character development aspects of martial arts training in hiring decisions. We bet you'll be glad you did.

CHAPTER FIFTY-SIX

ENTER THE DRAGON

"To a man utterly without a sense of belonging, mere life is all that matters. It is the only reality in an eternity of nothingness, and he clings to it with shameless despair."

– Eric Hoffer

Despite the fact that you have only one brain, you have three minds. Depending on how you count them, you may technically have more, or perhaps less, but for our purposes you have three. And the counting shall be three... oh, wait... We're talking about the human mind, the lizard mind, and the monkey mind.

Your human mind is thoughtful and aware, reasonable if not always purely logical. You are not in this mode nearly as often as you think you are, however. When you use your human mind, you weigh the costs and do the right things regardless of your emotions. You live up to your highest ideals.

Your lizard mind, ruled by your lizard brain, is older. Scientifically speaking, it is two almond-shaped amygdala located deep inside your head, forming a sort of mini-brain. As a species it has served well over the millennia to keep us alive, dealing with base imperatives like danger, hunger, and movement. When you are in your lizard mind, you move like an animal, like an athlete. It is pure. It can often be vicious and it is ruthless. It is older and baser than human concerns like justice or mercy...

In the middle is your monkey mind. We evolved from social primates—animals that lived in tight groups, and were completely dependent on their community for survival. Our interdependence drove an evolution toward social skills and social strategies to deal with conflict. Your monkey mind is concerned, always and obsessively, with what other people might think about you.

You are rarely in just your lizard mind. When absolute terror kicks in and you break out of the fight-flight-freeze and just act, it is a lizard thing. Sometimes a few feel it when they have trained for a long time and hit the zone, the state of *mushin* to use the Japanese terminology, where they can act with absolute grace yet without conscious thought. Many, today, only hit this zone playing video games, where they have trained to reflex on the controls and can play without registering exactly what they are pretending to do...

or caring who might see them doing it.

It is just as rare to be in your human mind. When you have done the right thing even though people you care about will be angry; when you have stood by the facts even though everyone said you were wrong... How often do you really do that, take that risk? When Galileo recanted the truth out of fear of the church, he gave up his human mind and did what a monkey would do.

As much as we are ever just in one of these three minds, it is most often the monkey. Obsessed with the tribe, with others, angsting over how other people really feel, worrying whether someone really likes us. Even silly things like following celebrity gossip are monkey brain (as a sidebar, on what world is it important who Angelina and Brad even are let alone what they are doing?). Concerns about whether you blend in enough or stand out too much, this is monkey stuff. The insecurity of an animal that needs a community, because it knows it is too weak to survive in the wild on its own, that's your monkey mind.

The monkey mind interacts with the other two obsessively. When a gunshot goes off and people start looking around to see what other folks are doing, that's the monkey mind. When you don't duck or hit the dirt because you are afraid of what others will think, that's the monkey mind too. And when your first instinct is to slam the door in a stranger's face and you don't because "that would be rude," well...

monkey mind. In all of these cases, people have been raped or tortured or killed because they were more worried about what others would think than they were about their own survival. That's how powerful the monkey is.

It's not a conscious choice, it's an instinctive response. The monkey mind interferes with the human mind as well. For example, writers struggle with their "inner critic," the voice constantly whispering to them to give up, that they aren't good enough, that they don't know enough to succeed. The monkey mind is just as concerned with being too special, too successful, as it is with being rude or looking silly. Being too good can also push you out of the tribe if it ignites others' jealousy (Salem Witch Trials anyone?). Monkeys die if they have to go it alone.

The same dynamic plays with every incident of hiding the truth or ass-covering or sucking up; the monkey wants to belong. And, that need to belong is more important than the truth... or even survival.

That is huge, because the monkey mind doesn't distinguish between physical death and humiliation or isolation. Any profound change in you, even learning a new skill, might terrify the monkey. It sees change as what some call "ego death." Your monkey mind constantly fights to keep you in your comfort zone, where nothing changes. No matter how much that comfort zone sucks to your human mind (when you don't live up to your potential; when you feel the shame of taking the easy way instead of the right way) or your lizard mind (and so people die rather than take the chance that fighting might be rude or running might seem cowardly). Your own monkey brain will fight you if what you need to do to survive might impact your social standing.

This impacts martial artists profoundly. When training becomes a hierarchical series of rituals it recreates the monkey tribe. Socially secure, everyone knows their places and what to do... but that's not really what martial arts is all about is it? When students are afraid to ask why or how something works, or when students continue to practice flawed technique because even though they can't make them work what they are doing looks right, then the monkey has won.

Martial arts should be about the human mind and the lizard mind, not the monkey. Developing an ethical understanding of force and violence, educating and training an animal body to new levels of efficiency, that's what martial arts should be. It's fundamentally about empowering students. When the training caters to the monkey mind, it robs the students of power. It cripples students who may, someday, need to do the right thing (human brain) with absolute efficiency (lizard brain) in order to survive. The monkey has no place in martial arts training.

When you silence the chattering monkey (meditation works for some, simply recognizing it for others) and get the human mind and lizard brain to work together in harmony, you build something new.

Something that uses the human abilities and virtues—thoughtfulness, righteousness, planning, goal-setting, and decision-making—with the deep abilities of the ancient lizard, efficiency, ruthlessness, and absolute focus.

And that is the rarest mind, the dragon mind. Enter the dragon!

Making it real...

For students and teachers alike it takes concerted effort not to get caught up in the monkey mind. Consider carefully where you train and why. Is the atmosphere conducive to thoughtful discussion rather than blind obedience? How do you allow for that without disrupting training with debate? There's no silver bullet here, but make a concerted effort to lock the monkey in his cage and train only humans and lizards. Done right you can build dragons in your *dojo*.

CHAPTER FIFTY-SEVEN

AWARENESS

"The ultimate value of life depends upon awareness and the power of contemplation rather than upon mere survival."

– Aristotle

When we hear some martial artist saying, "The first step in self-defense is being aware," we go into anaphylactic shock. Not really, but it does make us cringe. That phrase is the martial arts equivalent of the pointy-haired boss from the Dilbert comic strip telling you to, "Work smarter, not harder." It's worthless... absolutely worthless.

But then it continues with, "You need to look both ways before you put your keys in the car," and, "You need to have an escape route." Okay, all well and good, that's a start, but we want to take you a little further, make it a little more real. Gavin DeBecker's book, *The Gift of Fear*, presents two key points:

1) Trust your gut reaction
2) Criminals are clever and very good at what they do

Then he dives into the breakdown of those two points, demonstrating the permutations of criminal behavior, and carefully outlines the types and actions they might take. He instructs readers how to recognize pattern and form to give their gut reaction credence. At the simplest level, out instincts have been carefully honed over the millennia to recognize threats. It's what kept our ancestors alive, so why on earth wouldn't we listen to it now, the context may be different but the reaction much the same.

Just as CPAs know all the ins and outs of the tax code so that they can excel at their duties, criminals are adept at tricking the law abiding into falling for their schemes. We can't do taxes as well as our accountants and we can't break the law as effectively as professional criminals do. But, we can become and remain aware of their dirty tricks, learn how to spot their patterns.

How many times have you been to an event when you see or hear some yelling? Everybody looks and turns toward the disturbance, right? That is a disruption of pattern. If it isn't normal, pay attention, assess the threat, and determine whether or not it's directed to you. That's awareness.

This recognition of pattern is the beginning of wisdom. It helps awareness become more than just a buzzword.

Making it real...

Here is a drill you can do to help you get better at awareness by watching for small disturbances, finding what doesn't fit, what is slightly out of place, and then putting it in the context of the moment. Watch crowds. Any crowd will do, but crowds at concerts and sporting events are best as tempers tend to flare there. Look for sights, sounds, smells, movements, whatever; anything that's not normal. You can ask yourself a lot of questions, but the best one to ask is what every method actor in the world has been trained to ask, "What is my motivation?" See the disturbance and find the motive. Could the motive be violence toward another? Violence to protect oneself? Rage? Alcohol? Drugs? Every time you attend a large public event you should have an opportunity to practice your awareness skills, bringing them from a trite phrase of "paying attention" to a powerful weapon with which to keep you safe.

CHAPTER FIFTY-EIGHT

TRADITION AND BUNNY HOPS

"Real knowledge is to know the extent of one's ignorance."

– Confucius

Bunny hops, putting your hands behind your head and hopping around the *dojo* floor, is a longstanding tradition in classical martial arts training. And, it is horrifically bad for your knees. Several other exercises fall into that same category of "seemed like a good idea sixty years ago," but today we know that it is not. We know much more about physiology, the functions of the human body and its parts, than we did half a century ago. Further, we live longer than we used to which means that the practice of maintaining our bodies is even more important than it used to be.

Are you willing to live in pain for the rest of your life simply to follow tradition? In that vein we continuously look at the exercises we use to warm-up before class and have quietly dropped some of them over time. There's no sense in being bound by tradition when empirical evidence proves that an exercise is not getting the job done, and, in fact, may be causing injury.

Now that ought to be an easy thing to do. To drop or change an exercise because of evidence that it doesn't work, seems like a no-brainer right? The question then becomes, why is that so hard to do the same thing when it is an interpretation of a technique?

Look at it this way: We will drop an exercise like a hot potato if evidence proves that it might injure us. Why, then, will we not do the same when the evidence proves a self-defense technique might get me seriously hurt? All too often instructors joke about unrealistic *kumite*, yet they keep teaching them because "they're only tandem drills" or some other lame reasoning.

If it doesn't have true martial value, if it doesn't work against an unwilling opponent, someone bigger, stronger, meaner, or more vicious than the martial practitioner, why on earth are your teaching it? That makes you look like an idiot, and sets your students up to fail.

Making it real...

Is your hesitancy to drop a known interpretation that will get you hurt because of an allegiance to your instructor? The system you bought into? Or is it just a lack of really taking a look at what is being done? Examine the traditions you've blindly followed in light of modern experience. If it doesn't work find out why, perhaps it is due to lack of understanding, body type or psychological predilections, or some other legitimate reason, but if it's fundamentally flawed stop teaching it.

CHAPTER FIFTY-NINE

BLACK EYES AND MAT-RASH

"The people heard it, and approved the doctrine, and immediately practiced the contrary."

– Benjamin Franklin

The other day when I stood up off the mat I knew that I was going to be sporting some bruises from where my training partner had grabbed and twisted my *gi*. The guy I got up off of was looking back at me through a swollen eye, but we both had grins on our faces, because a quick cat and mouse game of *ne-waza* (ground work) had come to an end. The next day his eye was a little swollen and my upper arms and chest had some nice purple discolorations and a few scratches.

"Macho!" you might scream, upon reading this. "You idiots are doing nothing but being macho buttheads!"

Well, we would have to disagree obviously, but this leads to an important point. Here's the difference between being a macho butthead and a smart, hardworking practitioner: Nobody was hurt. We worked fast and strong, but nobody needed ice, or a wrap, or a doctor for that matter. And that is the difference. None of the minor rashes we had would stop us from competing that weekend in any sport.

Conversely if you were saying, "Yeah I would like to compete but I was training so hard that I separated my shoulder." Now *that* is macho BS and it deserves to be called out.

Injuries, accidents, and mishaps happen in contact sports, but training to the point of consistent and constant injury, that's just plain wrong. Does the National Football League train like that? Nope! In fact, we dare you to find any professional sports team that trains recklessly. You can't, because they don't (nor do collegiate teams for that matter). Money is on the line with the pros and that's the bottom line. They have to train hard, but smart, since injured players cannot contribute and if the best personnel are not able to take the field chances are good the team will not prevail.

The new concussion safety rules are a good example. The heads-up coaching certification is required at all levels from the pee-wee leagues all the way up through the NFL. It's a conscientious and mature response to player safety concerns.

You should be just as smart. A black eye and some

mat rash are part of fun training, true injury is not. Know the difference.

Making it real...

An important yet often overlooked requirement of holistic martial arts training is first aid. After all, if you are learning how to break someone shouldn't you know how to fix them too? Law enforcement, security, and military personnel get extensive first aid training. Martial artists should too. So, if you're not certified for at least basic first aid and CPR, go take a class. The American Red Cross and similar agencies offer outstanding training for a very minimal price. It not only gives you a leg up in emergencies, but also helps assure that you know enough to train more safely too. Oh, and make sure your first aid kit is up to snuff too—the one in your car, your house, and in your *dojo*.

CHAPTER SIXTY

TO BE A BLACK BELT

"It is good to have an end to journey toward; but it is the journey that matters in the end."

– Ernest Hemmingway

Years ago I was in Florida doing some training. On the wall of the school were huge, I mean three feet high kind of huge, words proclaiming, "My Goal is to be a Black Belt." I internally mocked that statement at the time.

"Geez," I thought, "You would think that they would be pushing something else, something that has real value. You know, skills, morals, values, wisdom, that kind of thing." Those big letters really hit me in the wrong way. They smacked faux dedication, affection, a marketing ploy. And, I was having none of it.

Now many years later I look back on that signage

through a new lens. There can be deep value to having such a declarative statement painted on the wall. Focus, affirmation, and a shared commitment. I don't have anything that huge on the wall of my *dojo* wall, but I do have something similar, smaller and in *kanji*—the word "perfection." This suits my school better than the big words painted on the wall yet the idea is still the same.

There is a Japanese proverb that states, "Vision without action is a daydream. Action without vision is a nightmare."

Looking back, I can see the wisdom of those big words in this axiom and feel a little foolish in my quick dismissal some twenty years ago.

Making it real...

Sometimes you need to write things down to make them real. The simple act of writing down, or of stating your aspirations aloud, can focus and ignite your will. If it's only in your head there's oftentimes less energy, lower stakes. After all, you're the only one who knows you didn't follow through. The public declaration, on the other hand, that's hard not to live up to. It's why many corporations make employees reaffirm their ethics programs in writing every year. So, what is your training goal? Who have you told about it? And, what steps will you take to assure it becomes real?

CHAPTER SIXTY-ONE

DECISION MAKING

"Calmness is the cradle of power."

– Josiah Gilbert Holland

Deliberate calm is a term used by pilots and astronauts to describe the ability of the mind, through training, to override an emotional response to an intense moment. Cops feel it, firefighters too, and you have as well. When you might ask? Well, a good example is when you have had to swerve to miss another car on the highway and you feel nothing but the moment. While you drive you drive to safety it is deliberate calm, total focus. Afterward when you're safe, you become a mess. And often do.

Simply put, this is what repetitive martial arts training attempts to bring to the practitioner, the ability to perform at a high level without conscious thought, to be in the moment, take care of business, and remain calm until the danger has past.

Here is a link to a four-minute explanation by author Jonah Lehrer of *How We Decide*: http://www.peterme. com/?p=746. We find his comments challenging and enlightening at the same time.

He states, for example, that the thought process that excels in the supermarket won't pass muster in the Oval Office. Natural selection has endowed us with a brain that is enthusiastically pluralist. Sometimes we need to reason through our options and carefully analyze the possibilities, while other times we need to listen to our emotions and gut instinct. The challenge then becomes knowing when to use each different style of thought—when to trust feelings and when to exercise reason.

Martial arts not only train the body, they also condition the mind. Pressure testing, sparring, and reality-based simulations help us reason through alternatives in relative safety so that we can make faster, better decisions when everything is on the line. Oftentimes that confidence carries over into other aspects of our lives—in business negotiations for example.

Lawrence recently bought a used car. While it's relatively easy to buy new cars online without haggling and assure you've gotten a good deal, say through the Costco auto program, that's simply not possible in the used car market. There's virtually always some kind of negotiation needed since the value of each individual vehicle is based on its mileage, condition, ownership, accident history, etc. Most people hate shopping for used cars, dreading dealing with high pressure sales people. Martial artists on the other hand, well, if the other guy isn't throwing a punch, wielding a knife, or pointing a gun, how much pressure can there truly be?

Making it real...

How has your martial art crossed over into your everyday life? If you're mental focus, clarity, and calm are greater in the face of adversity you're doing something right. If not, look for opportunities to explore those facets of the arts. It might be a seminar (or series of classes), a meditation regimen, or some sort of personal reading, research, and exploration, but whatever fits best don't miss out on the opportunity turn your training into something more than mere punching, kicking, and grappling. It can and should be a life-affirming experience.

CHAPTER SIXTY-TWO

SOUND LIKE A WUSS

"It bothers me when people equate niceness with being dull or wishy-washy. It makes me sound like a wuss."

– Tom Selleck

In the world where we celebrate the notorious we find actor Tom Selleck's comments refreshing and truthful. We also recognize his frustration. You see wolves respect power; well most of the animal kingdom does in fact. When we as humans carry that impression over from animal to human domain, niceness is seen as weakness. In perception being nice is often taken as a sign of subservience, of kowtowing. In fact, however, more often than not that perception is simply not true.

Niceness is the first act of stepping into the role of being human, of engaging people on a human level instead of simply having a human expression of an animal behavior. How does this apply to the martial arts? Through the rank or belt system.

Rank not only records achievement, it delineates and separates people. When superior ranks use that separation as a means of lording over the lower ranks, well that is not cool and the higher rank is... well not being a nice person. They are acting out a role of animal existence, a role of alpha wolf; at least they think they are. You see, "insecure" alphas lord over others, whereas true alpha wolves' primary role is to protect the pack. They're in charge because they are the biggest, toughest, wisest of the bunch, a positive force for the group. Insecure alphas, on the other hand, are so worried about being in charge that they are always fighting for position.

It works the same way in the animal world as it does in the human one.

Making it real...

If you are with a club, *dojo*, or job for that matter, where the superiors believe being, "firm, hard, and heavy-handed" makes them not a wuss, you might want to rethink your participation. That kind of behavior only gets people so far in life, and hitching your wagon to their behavior will eventually limit you as well. Being a nice person, someone who can defend him- or herself if necessary, that is a much more pleasant path to walk. And, not anything close to being a wuss. After all, the tougher you truly are the less you should feel a need to prove it.

CHAPTER SIXTY-THREE

MAKING PROMISES... AND KEEPING THEM

"Anything is better than lies and deceit!"

– Leo Tolstoy

Promises are not big in our book. We heard a lot of them: "Oh, I promise I'll send the pictures from the seminar." "I promise I'll pay you." "I promise this, I promise that, I promise something else..."

The question we have is, "Why do you need to promise? Isn't your word good enough?"

We grew up old school, back in the handshake days when a person's word meant a lot more than legalese scribbled on a piece of paper and it taints our perspective. Did you know that Ray Crock, founder of McDonald's corporation, didn't use written contracts when making deals with his suppliers?

He found the right people, aligned their goals, and relied on nothing more than handshakes to build a billion dollar business.

We meet a lot of people these days, and given all the proverbial irons we have in the fire, we tend do some form of business with a number of them. However, when we hear the words, "I promise" we tend to just write that person off. Seriously, we forget about it, because if they needed to promise that means they have not followed through in the past and are unlikely to do so now.

We're not trying to set ourselves up as some paragons of virtue. We have made more mistakes than there are stars in the heavens, well maybe not that many but certainly a lot. The point is that we take the "I promise" statement as a cue to just forget about whatever the other person just said. Perhaps it's just a turn of phrase, but in our experience more often than not it's an admission of dubious virtue—like the conman who always says "trust me"—this is someone making a promise they have no intent to keep.

Making it real...

It ought to go without saying, but when you give your word keep it. Actions speak far louder than words, and no matter what you say people will judge you by the actions you take. While all men and women should be upstanding citizens, martial artists ought to hold themselves up to an even higher standard. If you have children that ups the stakes even farther, as your kids usually emulate the behaviors you model for them. Consequently, if you can't, won't, or simply don't want to do something, don't promise someone that you will. Simple advice, but it can keep you out of a whole lot of trouble.

CHAPTER SIXTY-FOUR

BANKRUPTCY OF PURSE
OR BANKRUPTCY OF LIFE

"Life is either a daring adventure or nothing. Security does not exist in nature, nor do the children of men as a whole experience it. Avoiding danger is no safer in the long run than exposure."

– Helen Keller

Sterling Hayden (1916 – 1986) was an actor and author. At six feet five inches tall, his forte in acting was the Western. He also did several great film noir too. He was in *Dr. Strangelove*, *The Godfather*, and many other notable films. Hayden always considered acting a way financing his adventures. Read his words from his autobiography, *Wanderer*, and see if you find resonance with his comments:

To be truly challenging, a voyage, like a life, must rest on a firm foundation of financial unrest.

Otherwise, you are doomed to a routine traverse, the kind known to yachtsmen who play with their boats at sea... cruising, it is called. Voyaging belongs to seamen, and to the wanderers of the world who cannot, or will not, fit in. If you are contemplating a voyage and you have the means, abandon the venture until your fortunes change. Only then will you know what the sea is all about.

I've always wanted to sail to the South Seas, but I can't afford it.' What these men can't afford is not to go. They are enmeshed in the cancerous discipline of security. And in the worship of security we fling our lives beneath the wheels of routine—and before we know it our lives are gone. What does a man need—really need? A few pounds of food each day, heat and shelter, six feet to lie down, and some form of working activity that will yield a sense of accomplishment. That's all—in the material sense, and we know it.

But we are brainwashed by our economic system until we end up in a tomb beneath a pyramid of time payments, mortgages, preposterous gadgetry, playthings that divert our attention for the sheer idiocy of the charade. The years thunder by, the dreams of youth grow dim where they lie caked in dust on the shelves of patience. Before we know it, the tomb is sealed. Where, then, lies the answer? In choice. Which shall it be: bankruptcy of purse or bankruptcy of life?

Making it real...

Profound statements, huh? But, if you're anything like us Hayden's words get you thinking. Have we grown so attached to security that we're missing out on life? We're not advocating selling off all your worldly possessions and setting about to circumnavigate the globe with nothing more than a knapsack and a compass, but we are suggesting that oftentimes we stay in a lousy job, relationship, or situation simply out of fear of change. Examine your motivations. Are you missing out on something profound for lack of willingness to take the risk? Do you face a bankruptcy of purse or a bankruptcy of life?

CHAPTER SIXTY-FIVE

CULTURAL REASSURANCE

"A liar begins with making falsehood appear like truth, and ends with making truth itself appear like falsehood."

– William Shenstone

Okay, we are going to get a little hoity-toity here, but bear with us: It is nice when our peers tell us we are doing the right thing. We like it when we get cultural reassurance, a metaphorical nod in our direction that says, "That was well done, you're a good person."

However cultural reassurance is not always right. In fact, oftentimes it's as flexible as a Cirque du Soleil' contortionist. If, for example, we spend two years working on a wristlock, having our training partners honor that technique, being cooperative and everybody in the *dojo* behaving in that same pattern, we have a significant amount of cultural reassurance. We feel great about what we are doing, and soon we begin to believe it. We justify in our minds that the technique is rock-solid and others join in that dance of cultural reassurance.

So far so good huh? Not really...

Then the day comes where the person on the other end of the technique does not dance our dance, they have a far different culture... We are no longer reassured. In fact we are suddenly cracked wide open, crushed. We feel betrayed.

The question now becomes, "Should I be angry at myself or the culture that set me up for this failure?"

Pause for effect... you should blame yourself. The culture that you have subscribed to is going to do whatever it needs to do to propagate itself, including lie to you, it can't help it. That is what it does. You are responsible to yourself, for what you choose to believe and do.

Martial arts schools are bubble baths of cultural reassurance, warmly soaking each student in their own brand of comfort and truth. That doesn't mean that your school is wrong or leading you down a path of cultural reassurance, based on falsehoods, and lies. It means it is doing what it does and you need to decide for yourself what you are willing to accept.

Making it real...

Educate yourself. Study books and videos by experienced, no-nonsense practitioners like Loren

Christensen, Marc MacYoung, or Rory Miller. Two of the three are retired cops, whereas the third is a reformed bad guy. They have a low tolerance for BS because they actually had to use what they've learned to survive. Rory, in particular, does a fabulous job of showing the world for what it is, not what we wish it to be. Books like *Meditations on Violence*, *Facing Violence*, and *Scaling Force* can illuminate misconceptions in ways that few others are able to do.

CHAPTER SIXTY-SIX

ONE BAD APPLE DON'T SPOIL THE WHOLE BUNCH, GIRL

"See if you can catch yourself complaining, in either speech or thought, about a situation you find yourself in, what other people do or say, your surroundings, your life situation, even the weather. To complain is always non-acceptance of what is. It invariably carries an unconscious negative charge. When you complain, you make yourself into a victim. When you speak out, you are in your power. So change the situation by taking action or by speaking out if necessary or possible; leave the situation or accept it. All else is madness."

– Eckhart Tolle

"One bad apple don't spoil the whole bunch, girl." Recognize those lyrics? They're from *The Osmonds*. Yeah, we're old, and sadly prove it by remembering that hit by that toothy, bubblegum band of brothers from the early seventies. However, lyrics aside, a bad apple will spoil the whole bunch soon enough if it is not soon removed from the other apples. A little lesson from *The Osmonds*... and Mother Nature.

Any person who has been involved in sports or business can tell you about the person who is "Locker Room Poison," or "Water Cooler Gossip Poison."

Lou Piniella (a future member of the Baseball Hall of Fame) managed the Seattle Mariners baseball club from 1993 to 2003. There was a guy on the team during that time who became locker room poison. This player, his name is not important, was good, not great. He added to the team on the field with his play, but he talked out of turn to the press about what he saw as problems on the team... He was a gossip and it was not good.

Think the press ran with those stories? You bet they did. Did it take Lou Piniella long to figure out who the gossip was? No, no it did not take "Sweet Lou" long at all.

Oh, Piniella tried to fix the problem, but it was just this player's nature. Despite Lou's coaching, that guy kept talking to the press in negative ways about the games and the players. Not a man to put up with much of this sort of thing, Piniella then began to search for a replacement. As soon as this player hit a bad patch, he was pulled from the field and then quickly traded to get him off the bench and out of the baseball team's organization.

Lou Piniella removed the rotten apple as soon as he could to stop the rotting process. Despite the fact that the song says, "One bad apple don't spoil the whole bunch, girl," if Lou Piniella had written the next verse it would been something along the lines of, "Yeah, but he is out of my locker room as soon as possible." Skilled leaders recognize this bad apple phenomenon and address it quickly and with little mercy.

Making it real...

Are you the bad apple? Do you gossip, subvert the team/organization, talk people down behind their backs? We hope not, but if you find yourself guilty of that behavior it's no way to win friends or influence people. Knock it off! And, if you've got a bad apple in your midst see what you can do to change his or her outlook, but don't be afraid to let him/her go if the behavior doesn't change. Unaddressed such situations become toxic.

CHAPTER SIXTY-SEVEN

I WAS CHANGED
BY THE MARTIAL ARTS

"Experience teaches only the teachable."

– Aldous Huxley

It is rare that you have a conversation with somebody who has been in the martial arts for any length of time and not in some way have them relate to you that they are better for having trained in the arts. It really doesn't make that much difference, we have found, what form they have trained in. Good instructors, clear systems, and dedication are the cornerstones to a quality experience, and you get that with virtually any style or school.

There is another side of this formula, however, that often is not the most prominent and that is how the instructors are changed. It makes sense when you think about the formula. A student sees one instructor (or a small handful of them), whereas the instructor sees dozens, perhaps even hundreds of students. Take whatever the class number size is, add in changes that that inevitably occur as folks drop out or new ones sign up, and then multiply that times the number of months or years you've been teaching. We are changed in large and small ways by almost every student that we have had the opportunity to instruct.

Carl Jung said, "The meeting of two personalities is like the contact of two chemical substances: if there is any reaction, both are transformed."

We have had students die from terminal illnesses and others who have persevered despite having dysfunctional hip-sockets, severe scoliosis, or needing to pursue training whilst confined to a wheelchair. Mentally, we have looked into the eyes of the autistic, painfully bashful, dyslexic, and functional illiterate, had a glimpse of what the world looks like through their perspective. These people, they are the ones that have left and continue to leave the biggest impressions.

Everybody usually has something to contribute in this realm, yet the contrast between these folk's maladies and their effort is most striking. Often the gift they leave is far more profound than that of the natural athlete, the gifted martial artist, or flexibility of youth has the capability to leave.

Making it real...

Clearly the folks you train with, students and teachers alike, impact you. A bit of everyone rubs off, some leaving profound marks on your soul as they pass through the *dojo*. Have you taken a moment to thank your training partners? Sometimes we forget to say it, but heartfelt appreciation toward those who have made a difference is always in order.

CHAPTER SIXTY-EIGHT

BROAD OR DEEP

"As a rule, I am very careful to be shallow and conventional where depth and originality are wasted."

– Lucy Maud Montgomery

One evening after training at the *Jundokan* International *dojo* I was invited to Chinen *Sensei's* home where we and talked, oddly enough, about karate. After about a half hour or so, Chinen just looks at me and says, "You teach too much; you need to go deeper into what you have."

What he was saying was simple and often overlooked. Something that is designed for everyone rarely reaches anyone. Come again? I was teaching too much material, and as a result studying too broadly... My art was suffering, my students were suffering, and none of us even realized it.

Taking his advice, I returned home and went to work. I pared down the *dojo* syllabus, stripping off much of what had been added over the years by so many instructors before me. A codified set of movements, officially named and written into the canon of the art, I chipped away at them all.

After the list was completed, I dove into the forms for more study. Oddly, the deeper I studied the farther the bottom of the information receded from me. All of a sudden, I was deep and not broad. My focus was now not so much on pattern as it was on the simple turning of my knee, the pushing of a foot, or the alignment of my spine.

And I am stronger for it.

Making it real...

A huge challenge with many martial styles, especially nowadays, is the vast amounts of information that must be understood, put in to practice, and mastered. In the old days, back before World War II, most karate students in Okinawa learned a fundamental form, say *sanchin* or *naihanchi*, and one or two more *kata*—those that best fit their personality and body type. Only the master's heir apparent would learn the entire system. It wasn't until after the war when so much knowledge was lost that the curricula were opened up to everyone. While this helped assure that the arts would not be lost, it opened up a host of other problems. For example, while it may be possible to deeply know and understand a dozen *kata*, there's virtually no way that anyone could master the 70-something forms that some schools teach. We assert that in order to truly make use of your art it's better to deep than broad. Audit what you teach, what you practice, and determine whether or not you've cast your net too wide.

CHAPTER SIXTY-NINE

SPREAD IT AROUND

"A bone to the dog is not charity. Charity is the bone shared with the dog, when you are just as hungry as the dog."

– Jack London

Martial artists are different. We have said it before and will undoubtedly say it again. As martial artists we expect more from ourselves, to be nice, treat people well, not become bullies or use our training for nefarious purposes. But what if that's not our inclination? What if we see that maybe that higher decency is not our true nature, that there's something we need to keep in check? Well, that's actually a good thing, seeing a less-than-flattering aspect of ourselves, accepting the problem, and addressing it.

We've both had a similar challenge in our youth. It took us a long time to see that often we did not listen very well, that we were more concerned with getting our point across than with fully engaging in equal conversations with others. Sometimes we had the kooky idea that what was said didn't really mean anything, or that the new policy was for other people, or we simply got impatient and jumped in before hearing the whole thing through.

Being the far-from-perfect individuals that we are, it took several smacks upside our heads to get the point across... we needed to do something different.

Eventually it sunk in. Then, we suddenly decided to change our behavior. Yup, just like that. The trigger was different in each instance, but we both made the exact same decision. We sought out articles on how to listen effectively, read a few books, took a class or two, and applied what they said. We didn't try to apply the things we'd learned, we made the decision and then made it happen.

What? Really?! Just like that, you can change? Yes, just like that. We did change. Here's why: As humans what we think about, we do. What we do long enough becomes habit. And, what becomes a habit changes us. It really is that simple and, perhaps, that profound... Decide, do, become.

We're not that special. You can do the same thing too.

Making it real...

If you have something that you would like to change, apply that martial artist difference we all possess, that drive that makes us keep coming back to the *dojo*, reading everything we can about the arts, going to seminars, and squeezing the last bit of information we can from any source we can get our hands on. Repetition and, well... more repetition. Take that desire and intensity for martial arts and spread it around into other aspects of your life. There's no downside to becoming a better person.

CHAPTER SEVENTY

TIME AND TIME MANAGEMENT

"Time is what we want most, but what we use worst."

– William Penn

We both have insanely busy schedules, balancing family, jobs, teaching, writing, and more, a whole host of responsibilities any one of which could wipe out all our free time if we let it. Here's a little trick that helps us get more done. Each year, sometime in November, we write down our goals for the forthcoming year. They are broken down into three categories: mental, physical, and spiritual. We then put three things, sometimes less, but never more than three, in each of those categories. These goals are written on a three-by-five index card and stuck on our desks.

We try to make these three items specific, but we don't restrict ourselves. Sometimes a general statement is fine, but you should move down through the general statement to find its core and create an action that you can really wrap your hands around. Here's an example, riffing off the previous chapter:

We have started with "Be more patient."

Okay, that's a laudable goal, but it's challenging to put in action. This brings up the follow-on question, "How is patience demonstrated?"

There are a lot of good answers to that, but we chose to go with the Steven Covey principle, "Seek first to understand, then to be understood."

So, perhaps the card says, "Patience; listen more, speak less." The wording doesn't matter so long as it resonates with you. After all, it's your goal— personalize it.

This list doesn't have to be aligned with character development either, we just used that by way of example. It might also include something simple like, "Submit [New Book Title] to the publisher by September 1st." You get the picture. We chose November to write down our yearly goals because our birthdays happen to fall into that month, but this could be done in January as a sort of New Year's resolution or, frankly, any month you choose.

The point is that when you build a plan and monitor your progress the chances of successfully reaching your goals increase significantly. And, importantly, the odds of delving into time-wasting tangents that inhibit successful accomplishment of your true goals are greatly reduced.

Making it real...

Try our approach. Using a 3x5 card, list your goals for the next year. After all, goals not written are not real. Then, keep them in front of you. You'll be surprised how much you can accomplish if you dedicate your time toward disciplined pursuit of your goals.

CHAPTER SEVENTY-ONE

SOCIETY OF SQUEALERS

"Responsibility is the price of freedom."

– Elbert Hubbard

CenturyLink Field in Seattle is the home of the Seattle Seahawks football team. From time to time college games are played there as well. If you have ever attended a game at that venue you've probably noticed a sticker on the back of the chair in front of you that reads, "Make this game experience PG; if anyone is ruining your enjoyment, send a text message to..."

Think of all the messages we encounter during our daily routine. On Interstate 5, for example, a sign says, "Report litter bugs. Call..." Another reads, "Report HOV lane violators. Call..."

We really don't want to get all wrapped up in the argument that folks shouldn't be offensive or litter or whatever, that's not the point. We simply find the whole idea that folks are being encouraged to anonymously squeal on their fellow citizens to be abhorrent and for two reasons:

- First, the aspect of anonymity. We are just not fans of that. Sure, it has its role, but everywhere on everything? Cheezy Crispits! Isn't one of our founding principles the ability to face one's accuser? Anonymous squealing feels all Soviet-like.

- Second, and this is the most important point we really want to make here, this type of behavior does not give people power, it relocates it. It takes power from one person and gives it to others.

You relinquish the human interaction and the sovereignty to act for yourself. Instead of turning around and saying, "Hey, stop dropping the F-bombs; my kids don't need to hear that," you instead sit hunched over your QWERTY key pad and start squealing. Nah, that is not for us. We vastly prefer standing up and resolving problems face-to-face. It helps eliminate misunderstandings, while leading to greater accountability, civility (if handled right, of course), and responsibility.

Do we think those signs and policies should be removed or replaced? In an ideal world yes, but that horse has long left the barn so our opinions here mean little.

We had conversation with Marc "Animal" MacYoung (if you don't know who he is, his website is www. nononsenseselfdefense.com), the subject being the above points regarding squealing, anonymity, and giving away power. Marc listens thoughtfully, then says, "Sure, but the third part you left out is important."

He went on to explain what squealing does as a societal institution. It creates a servant class. It's almost like the scene in the movie *Tropic Thunder* where Tom Cruise as a Hollywood producer commands the key grip, via satellite, to punch the director for him and the key grip does it. We laugh because it is seems outlandish, but is it really?

Back to that seatback at CenturyLink Field telling us we squeal on somebody who is ruining our game-watching experience. How about we put on a toga, sit in the Roman Coliseum, and command our servants to remove a supporter of the blues (us being green) for ruining our sporting event? Is it any different? The servant is in our employ, our hands stay clean.

Yes Marc was right. We'd never thought of it that way. He went a little further by asking the question, "What is going to happen to these people when they don't have a servant to do their dirty work? What happens then, when never having experienced confrontation they are suddenly faced with something they need to act on directly?"

So, we add number three to our list above:

 ♦ Thirdly, squealing makes sure you never develop
   conflict resolution skills of your own as you hide
   behind the pinafore of authority.

As a result of squealing we are raising a generation
of individuals who have no skills in judging threats.
Their ability to measure (notice we didn't say
confront) is never developed because somebody
else, the servant class, is paid to do the dirty work, to
brush up against the threat.

Making it real...

Own your own dirty work. Yup, that simple... and that
difficult. Society makes it very easy to anonymously
report troubles to the authorities, to have someone
else do the hard things so that your hands stay clean.
So that our feelings aren't at risk. Man up (and that
includes you too, ladies). If you've got problems with
others deal with them head-on. Violence flows along
a communication continuum, so conflict resolution
skills are instrumental for keeping you safe.

CHAPTER SEVENTY-TWO

HARD EARNED WISDOM

"Creativity takes courage."

– Henri Matisse

One of the challenges faced by martial artists is how to be successful in their technique. That is to say, the judoka wants to throw a person to the ground, while the karateka wants to land the perfect strike. More often than not, forcing a technique is unsuccessful. Too much muscle, not enough skill, and often frustration makes a formula for failure.

Which brings us to a real-world example of how to get what you need done... Seattle, Washington where we live, is a very poorly run city. There is no need to belabor this chapter with numerous examples of ineptitude except for this one, because it is funny, factual, and demonstrates ingenuity and creativity, all of which make for good martial arts technique.

Because of a traffic reroute, a local neighborhood had cars using their residential streets to avoid traffic lights during the morning and afternoon commutes. The result of this was a large number of vehicles traveling on side streets that were never meant to handle them, cars and trucks going faster than they should and endangering families, kids, pets, cars pulling out of driveways, you name it.

All-in-all, this traffic created a generally bad situation, so the neighborhood petitioned the city to install speed bumps. The long and the short of the story is that the city denied their request. So, in an effort to protect their neighborhood, the leaders of that community bought their own speed bumps and spent a weekend installing them. City officials, upon hearing of these newly installed speed bumps sent a work crew out about a week later to the neighborhood to remove them.

Now we are not really getting into all of the justifications involved in this situation, but we think that something one man told a reporter who was covering the story was very wise. He suggested that instead of spending the money to install speed bumps they should have just used a pick and a shovel and made a couple of potholes, essentially making a negative speed bump, because the city has a horrible record of road repair... problem solved.

In the same vein we try to do our best to apply a little creativity, like the guy who suggested potholes instead of speed bumps, and be as clever as we can when it comes to our martial arts. Creativity in the martial arts should be cultivated.

Making it real...

Scenario training is great for exercising creativity. For example, Rory has a drill where he gives striking mitts or handheld pads to practitioners to hold onto, telling them that the pads are their infant children. Then, he starts the drill, giving instructions which invariably cause everyone to fight while simultaneously trying to hold onto their "children." Participants think that the purpose of the drill is to see how they can battle with a handicap, using only one arm instead of two, yet the real purpose is to see how well participants think through the situation they face. If that was a real baby they were holding onto our bet is that universally they'd flee from danger rather than moving to engage, but in every instance we've seen that drill everyone gleefully moves forward to fight... and fails the drill. Use scenarios like this, things that get folks thinking outside the proverbial box. Our minds are our greatest weapons; they need to be honed far more than our bodies.

CHAPTER SEVENTY-THREE

PERSONAL PRACTICE

"Practice is the hardest part of learning, and training is the essence of transformation."

– Ann Voskamp

Years ago, I arrived at the *dojo* early and my instructor was working on some techniques on the heavy bag over in the corner. The first thing I noticed was that he looked like he was working a technique that had recently been taught but he was doing it in a much different way than I had seen. He worked the technique a little bigger, more global, more fluid, and it look kind of crazy compared to what I had been recently taught. As soon as he saw me, he stopped his training... stopped cold.

We went on with the class; however, the moment clearly stuck with me. I told one of the senior students about my experience and why *Sensei* stopped training, "Why did the instructor stop? I wanted to see what he was doing?"

Well, I come to find out it was his personal practice, the time where he would explore a technique or application that he was emphasizing in his training at the moment. Completely personal, it has nothing to do with me. The point was, I should not copy it nor should I believe that I have seen some "secret" technique that would make a profound difference in my training or a street application.

You see, my instructor was built very differently than me. I am short, stocky, and stronger than he is. He was exactly the opposite, tall, lanky and limber. My instructor's personal training was about his body type, not mine. If I had attempted to copy his technique from his personal training, well, it wouldn't fit me.

Think of it as trying to put a Toyota part on a Ford car. Depending on what it is you might be able to make the Toyota part fit the Ford with a lot of work, but it's just never going to be quite right. Karate techniques are much the same. Sure, you *can* make it work, but should you?

Making it real...

When you see an advanced practitioner working on something, whether it's your instructor or someone teaching a seminar, and especially if that person does not share your body type or have your temperament, you might ask yourself, "How can I make that work for me?" Explore it from that end, instead of by rote. Mimicry is an excellent beginning, but not a permanent path.

CHAPTER SEVENTY-FOUR

KILL THE MESSENGER... AND ESPECIALLY THE MESSAGE

"The happiness of your life depends upon the quality of your thoughts. Therefore, guard accordingly, and take care that you entertain no notions unsuitable to virtue and reasonable nature."

– Marcus Aurelius

Many years ago, I was at a seminar and the instructor stood up in front of the class, shredded a local newspaper, and threw it to the ground. She said, "Quit reading this garbage!"

Honestly, the first thing that went through my mind was, "How am I supposed to know what is going on?" She proceeded to explain that it was all negative and then turned her vitriol toward television. At that time, I was so immersed in the dance of the media that I just thought she was being crazy, kooky in her rejection of it.

Since I am not always fast on the uptake, I rejected her comments just as she had dismissed the newspaper and television. A few years later, I found myself on her program. My television is now a monitor that I salvaged from a failing business. It gets no reception and I do not have it hooked up to cable. Newspaper subscriptions have long since lapsed.

At first, it was difficult. I was not able to have conversations with people about what happened on TV last night, nor was I hyper-knowledgeable about the local and world news. Honestly, it took me a year, maybe a year-and-half to break the hold the media had on me. However, when that tight-fisted grip was broken I found myself happier, more relaxed, and healthier.

"Really?" you say, "Happier, relaxed, and healthier?" Yes! Much more, thank you very much. I have found that I devote more time to reading, writing, martial arts, and spending time with friends and family, and all of those things I do with far more joy.

If I could make one recommendation to you it would be to get rid of your television, not physically, but kill the broadcast. Order movies and films from the library, Netflix, Amazon, or your local video store (if they're still in business); fill your mind with good stuff, fun stuff, or educational programming. Drill down into a subject and study. Use your television as a tool to your advantage; don't become enslaved by it.

Making it real...

Your choices in what you consume can determine your tone in life. We're not necessarily advocating killing your television, even Kris who no longer owns one watches football, but we are recommending that you use it wisely. The same thing goes for any other form of information, entertainment, etc. There are only so many hours in the day. Consider thoughtfully how you use them.

CHAPTER SEVENTY-FIVE

AN ODD COMBINATION OF EMOTIONS

"Transitions themselves are not the issue, but how well you respond to their challenges!"

– Jim George

I had been away from the judo *dojo* for a while and in that time my *sensei*, Kenji Yamada, had retired. A two-time national grand champion, he was now an old man. Yes, an old man. His family was very supportive in that they helped him transition to a Japanese assisted- living home in Seattle. He is doing well, but as his oldest son, when asked about his father's health, said, "He is slowing down."

Yamada *Sensei* taught more people judo than I might ever meet in my life; he was at the Seattle Dojo twice a week for over forty-five years, and taught at the Bellevue Boys & Girls Club too. So there I was standing alone in the upstairs changing room for black belts (they segregate the *yudansha* and *mudansha*, black belts and non-black belts). As I started changing, I saw peeking out from under a *gi* hanging on the pegged wall a red and white *obi*. It was Yamada *Sensei*'s *akashiro* (eighth-degree) black belt.

I looked again closer, and bent over to read the name on the belt. I shifted from side to side to focus, looking but not touching it. Yes, there I could see the two *kanji* embroidered on the end of the belt that formed the word for "Mountain Rice Paddy;" yes, it was *Sensei*'s belt and his uniform *gi*. As I stood there for a moment, bare-chested and hanging onto my judo pants' ties, I realized that Yamada *Sensei* never quit. *Sensei* was coming back; his last night at the *dojo* wasn't his last night, at least not in his mind.

After a moment, I started tying my pants and turned to put on my *gi* top. I felt a strange combination of sadness for a time passed and an appreciation of a last lesson left by an amazing teacher. Sometimes the deepest lessen is not planned, but lived.

◇◇◇

On April 10, 2014, not long after this chapter was written, Kenji Yamada passed away at the age of 90. Born an American citizen, raised in Japan, and interned during World War II, his unassuming dogged determination and commitment to the art of judo brought him two United States grand championships in the 1950s and the admiration of countless students, the authors among them. His commitment to the art bettered countless thousands of lives. He is survived by 9 children, 15 grandchildren, and one great grandchild. His obituary can be found here: http://www.legacy.com/obituaries/seattletimes/obituary.aspx?pid=170819931

Making it real...

Kris and Lawrence trained with *Sensei* Yamada and were both profoundly impacted by the experience. Whether they do so intentionally or not, everyone who teaches martial arts leaves a legacy. What will yours be? Take a moment to look back to the instructor who found something in you that you never knew existed. Look to how he or she was able to light your flame. They used their fire didn't they? Pay it forward. Don't try too hard to copy their methods, but do emulate their intent.

CHAPTER SEVENTY-SIX

MADONNA VS. DESCARTES

"Try not to become a man of success, but rather try to become a man of value."

– Albert Einstein

No, not *the* Madonna. We're talking about is the pop icon Madonna and her book from 1992 titled *Sex*. A controversial book at the time, it featured strong adult content but is pretty much lame, in today's vernacular. Then you have René Descartes the (1596 –1650), an influential French philosopher, mathematician, scientist, and writer.

Madonna strumpeted (to make up a word) around in skimpy outfits singing popular songs, whereas Descartes changed the world. He is often called the "Father of Modern Philosophy." Drop into a used book store, however, and you can find Madonna's book for sale somewhere in the fifteen dollar price range whereas you'll only have to shell out a whopping 75 cents for Descartes' *Discourse on Method* or *Meditations on First Philosophy*.

It's harder to read Descartes, and there are no salacious pictures, but our real point here is price versus value. The bookstore is going to sell books for whatever price the marketplace will bear, selling what it considers more valuable for a higher price and what it considered of less valued, well, for less. That's economics 101, right?

Buying two books by Descartes for less than two bucks, that's easy. If they're not in your local brick and mortar store, you can find them cheap in the Amazon marketplace or other online emporium. Reading his words, listening to his thoughts, and trying to grasp what he is telling us, it's slow going. It takes work. But, it makes us feel like thieves who stole from a bookstore something that did not know what they had. Or did they?

The world values the simple and the prurient.

Making it real...

What do you value? Much like Madonna's books and videos, an awful lot of practitioners are drawn to flash and extravaganza in the martial arts. Take for example, the patch-laden, multi-colored Rex-Kwon-Do *gi* (it's a movie stereotype, obviously, but one we have encountered often enough in real life), the commercialized MMA competition with bikini-clad ring babes, or the glittering weapons competitions featuring flashy, made-up forms that have little if any utility. Do these trappings diminish the arts? They certainly can and often do, but what really matters is whether or not such things further your goals, enhance your training. What are you training for, shape or substance?

CHAPTER SEVENTY-SEVEN

WELCOME
THE AMAZING RANDI

"Frisbeetarianism is the belief that when you die, your soul goes up on the roof and gets stuck."

– George Carlin

The Amazing Randi is a paranormal debunker who spends his time immersed in controversy. He challenges people's beliefs, strongly held notions. And, he debunks charlatans.

Challenging beliefs and what is assumed true is a divisive stance to take. You have on the one hand those who are angry that he has challenged their convictions or perceptions. On the other hand, you have those who laud Randi for his efforts. As a result, you get divisiveness, anger, and attacks— personal and public—flying hither and yon. At the end of the day, people are dug in like World War I trench warfare.

Controversy aside, every martial arts organization needs an Amazing Randi. Such a person provides a service that keeps the organization on course, fresh, and real. We have one and you should get one too... and listen to them.

These are the things he says, "I don't think it works like that, prove it to me." "Isn't that guy a little too aggressive?" "I don't get a good vibe off that person." "That seminar wasn't very good because..."

Now before you think this person is all negative, he isn't. He wants the facts, the truth, the reality of the moment. He knows that he can speak freely and that we will listen, really listen, to what he has to say. He makes us explain better, get answers, and think about the direction of the *dojo*.

While we always welcome his comments and thoughts, we do not always agree with him. Nevertheless, he is insightful, thoughtful, and serves well in his role of "The Amazing Randi of the *Dojo*." The *dojo* is much stronger, the instructors more grounded, for having him as a member.

Making it real...

Do you have an Amazing Randi in your midst? Oh, you probably do, but you may or may not have created an atmosphere where he or she feels comfortable bringing concerns to your attention. Turn your ear in that person's direction and listen. Look for the truth in good, constructive criticism.

CHAPTER SEVENTY-EIGHT

I DO MY KARATE
THE OLD FASHIONED WAY

"Without tradition, art is a flock of sheep without a shepherd. Without innovation, it is a corpse."

– Winston Churchill

You have taken that little sliver of your life you call your martial art and enshrined it, placed in stasis circa [insert the date of your founder's death here]. You might as well take all of your life and move it back to that time, right? It only follows that if you are willing to freeze that tiny sliver of your life in, say 1901, you should freeze the rest too.

Forget about, modern medical and physiological advances. No television, no computer, no Internet; bring back polio or rubella! And prop-driven planes with open cockpits are just around the bend, so for the next few years enjoy the train.

Look, you can be as progressive or orthodox as you want to be when it comes to the arts, however time is a continuum, people grow, advance, changes fall away and come together.

When we put on a suit and tie, we do it because it is the excepted practice for conservative business attire. It shows respect and formalness. We wear a traditional white *gi* and *kuri obi* (black belt) in the *dojo* for the very same reasons. It is the accepted attire for the circles in which we run.

However, when it comes to our art, we honor the tradition while being open to new ways of training, new interpretations of forms and techniques. It's part of keeping a martial art alive. The masters always took something established and added something new, and there will be others along the lineage who will leave the mark of their genius on the art as well.

It's all about balance. The masters of the martial arts are certainly to be revered. They've earned that veneration with the legacies they've built, systems and styles that remain relevant today because they worked well enough to stand the tests of time. Consequently, exploring new ways and interpretations that may differ with tradition should always be done with respect and careful consideration. But consider, we must. The tools and ideas our modern era has brought to the martial arts don't kill the traditions; they keep our traditions alive, assuring that they will be relevant and meaningful for years to come.

Here's an example: Classical martial systems were developed long before the advent of modern medicine. In those days, any injury sustained from a fight could be catastrophic. Knowing that the shorter the fight, the lower the chance of debilitating injury, the ancient masters built systems designed to stop adversaries as quickly and ruthlessly as possible.

The challenge is that the very same applications that may have kept you safe in the feudal times have limited utility today. It is not that they don't work, but rather that they work so well that they can only be used in certain situations. The brutal beat-down you deliver on the other guy might well save your life, but in the wrong circumstances it can also land you in jail.

When much of what we practice today was first invented, the modern rule-of-law and associated legal repercussions did not exist. Consequently, practitioners today cannot merely learn techniques, we must also understand the circumstances under which using them is appropriate. Without this vital context, we in essence train ourselves to wind up in jail.

Making it real...

Blind adherence to traditions of the art does no good. Review the curricula with a jaundiced eye. Question, probe, seek deeper understanding of the whys and wherefores, not just the what and how. If changes are warranted don't be afraid to evolve. Honor the past, build the future.

CHAPTER SEVENTY-NINE

THE GOOD PEOPLE

"We cannot live only for ourselves. A thousand fibers connect us with fellow men; and among those fibers, as sympathetic threads, our actions run as causes, and they come back to us as effects."

– Herman Melville

"Hey, I was up in your neck of the woods," said Big Jon Crain, an *Isshin-Ryu* karate practitioner. "I was up in the Okanogan and looking for a *dojo* to work out at. I walked into one and who was running it but Dan Keith!"

Jon taught us how to break rocks with our hands. Dan and Kris had trained together back in the early eighties, now these two connected. When Dan walked into the *taekwondo dojang* he said, "Jon what are you doing here?" They had met at *Martial University*, a now-defunct annual seminar that Kris used to run. Dan had Jon teach a weapons form to his students while he was practicing there.

Earlier in the week Kris had dinner with Matt Stone and a Vince Hardy (*YiLi Chuan kung fu*) and found out that they had hooked up with Lawrence to do a fundraiser for a very ill teenage boy. A couple days before that, when picking up his kid at the *dojo* one of our student's parents said, "I train with *Sifu* Dejesus. I'm in your latest book!" Sure enough, he was right there; we'd done a photo shoot at *Sifu* Dejesus' school.

What makes this work—karate, taekwondo, kung fu—how is it all linked up? Jon would likely say that it was *Martial University*, that these people all had been on the floor and trained together. We'd assert that it is simply good people meeting good people. Each person mentioned is an open-minded seeker in the arts. That's chewy goodness in our book. Not one of them has forsaken his or her base art, yet not one of them is threatened by another's art either. And, not one of them has an agenda other than the martial arts.

Here are the keys to having a strong and open architecture where folks of various styles can come together and learn:

- Little ego. Everybody needs an ego to survive, but can you make it small enough and pleasant enough to be around?

- Active listening. Are you learning or broadcasting? If you mouth is open, other than to ask a question, chances are good that you aren't learning.

- ◆ Good manners. If you would not behave that way at a dinner party then don't do it at the *dojo*.

- ◆ Laughter. Each one of these people has a good sense humor about the world and about themselves.

Every person mentioned in this post follows these basic guidelines. If asked they might suggest a small addition or modification to the list, but frankly we suspect they don't even think about it, because it is just part of them. That's what makes them good people—good to know, good to train with, and generally just, well, good.

Making it real...

Being open to others and letting them share their experience is a great way to broaden your life. This is true not only for martial arts, but for just about anything. Think about the folks you hang around. Do they add or subtract from your existence? After you interact do you feel energized and refreshed or drained? Value your time and your social interactions; seek out the good people.

CHAPTER EIGHTY

MAGIC AND KARATE

"I'm not upset that you lied to me, I'm upset that from now on I can't trust you."

– Friedrich Nietzsche

Magic and karate are similar in many ways. Being successful at either requires practice and hard work. To do magic, you have to get up off the couch, go to the magic store, buy the magic trick, and then practice, practice, practice, until the motions become seamless, until you can do it without conscious thought. Same with karate—get up off the couch, find a teacher and practice. A lot.

When magic is performed, there are two kinds of spectators. The first group is made up of those who enjoy the experience, the pageantry of the show, and the surprise of the trick. To them it's entertainment.

The second audience is comprised of those who scream, "I know how that was done!" "I saw that." And the ever popular, "Seen it before... yawn."

Those same people that scream the "I know..." phrase are the same people who aren't successful at the martial arts. They always assume that a great magic trick or a powerful karate move is really the result of some secret, easy to learn "trick." They believe there's a shortcut, a ploy, some method other than hard work and practice that makes things work. They are always looking for shortcuts—cheats that give them an edge without any true effort on their part. And they will always search in vain.

There is no special shortcut.

The simple fact of the matter is that magic tricks only work because of practice and hard work on the magician's part. Unsurprisingly, karate is the same. So is life. There are no shortcuts to things worth having.

Making it real...

Continuous practice... It's the paradox of time, right? It's tough to find the time to practice, yet without practice we cannot improve. Here's the deal, however, we all have more time than we think we do, maybe not in one big block but in lots of small increments—assuming we find creative ways to practice a little each day. When's the last time you stood in a karate stance while brushing your teeth, did calisthenics while watching television, or performed a visualization drill while sitting on the bus? Grab a moment here, a minute there, whatever you can find, and practice.

CHAPTER EIGHTY-ONE

MIND YOUR OWN BUSINESS, PUNK!

"I don't even call it violence when it's in self-defense; I call it intelligence."

– Malcolm X

At a bank with my son and one of his friends one afternoon, a young (22-ish) guy starts going off on the teller. He is raising his voice and his buddy is getting in on the action as well. Apparently, they are trying to cash an out-of-state, third-party check using expired identification or something.

The teller, overwhelmed by the aggressiveness of the two young men, calls the bank manager and the dance continues. Now the young guys start to use their go to tools, they start ripping loudly into the two bank employees with a bunch of obscenities.

The two young men are having some success; people are clearly feeling threatened and uncomfortable.

I turn to them, separated by a fat velvet rope, and say, "Hey, I've got kids here..." and before I can finish he spits out at me. "Shut your f*#king mouth, punk, this is none of your business."

"You made it my business when my kids can hear it," I respond. And, the monkey dance is ignited... It has turned into a group-grope, a three point monkey dance with the two young punks, the two bank employees, and me.

Now here is where it gets weird. The manager, who has just had his teller verbally assaulted as well as himself, turns to me, a fourteen-year account holder and says, "Sir you need to leave the bank." Now, I am incredulous at his ineptness, but stay calm and reply, "I am the one person who is protecting you and your clients from being assaulted. I suggest you call 9-1-1 right now."

The manager looks at me with an, "Oh, good idea" coming across his face. He reaches for the desk phone and starts dialing. The mouthy guy who was trying to cash the check, well, he told me that it was a good thing he had to go; otherwise he was going to do something to my punk ass. And he storms out.

As the teens are wont to say, "Whatever..."

The moral of the story?

When the monkey dance begins, there is no perspective, no rational thought. It's about status and show. The guys in the bank wanted to throw-down despite the fact that there were who knows how many closed-circuit video cameras capturing everything they did. Oh, and the bank manager is holding at least one of their drivers licenses in his hands. These guys are most likely in possession of a bad or stolen check, but that doesn't seem to matter either.

Not rational thinking, not even a little. But then again, that's how the monkey dance goes. I almost fell into it too, but ultimately let my human mind prevail.

People who use violence as a tool will oftentimes bypass socially acceptable procedures regardless of setting or context. In certain segments of society having a reputation, a "rep," can be very valuable, leading others to treat the person more respectfully for fear of his "going off" on them. The challenge is that for someone to be truly feared and respected it can't be a bluff, they need to earn it through action, and they may feel a need to do something well beyond the bounds of normal, acceptable behavior. It's still social violence rather than predatory because it is designed to develop status for the aggressor, but it doesn't always seem that way for those who are on the receiving end of it.

Face, status, reputation. This is your monkey.

Making it real...

Anger and fear are the primary emotions that cause conflict or disagreement to escalate into violence. When a person is locked into their monkey brain they are incapable of thinking rationally, hence unlikely to back down from any challenge that might cause them to lose face. The fear is social. And it is also real, at least at that particular moment. Change the context to break the cycle, find a face-saving way out. "Man, if we did fight, you'd probably kick my ass. Let's just skip that step and have a beer." You get the idea...

CHAPTER EIGHTY-TWO

IF YOU JUST SWALLOW EVERYTHING

"Three things cannot be long hidden: the sun, the moon, and the truth."

– Buddha

Break the *bunkai* (application)—take it out and break it. See if you can make the application fail. In fact, if you are not trying to break the *bunkai* then you are a lazy martial artist. Yup, we just called you a name: Lazy. If you accept everything that is taught to you, carte blanche, then you are brainwashed too. Just sayin'...

We had to laugh at the trailer for Ben Stein's movie *Expelled*. You may or may not recognize his name, but you probably know Stein from the movie *Ferris Bueller's Day Off*. His famous line, "Bueller, Bueller?"

delivered in his infamous deadpan, dry monotone. Or from his television show *Win Ben Stein's Money*. What you may not know is that Stein was also a speechwriter for United States Presidents Richard Nixon and Gerald Ford. He's a famous author and financial advisor too.

In the teaser for his movie, Stein is sitting in the back of the classroom, dressed as a schoolboy. This, of course, is funny in its' own right, an elderly, speechwriter and financial adviser dressed up as like Angus Young. Stein leans out from the back row and speaks to the teacher:

Ben Stein, "Excuse me, how did life begin in the first place?"

Teacher, "Mr. Stein you have the same question every time..."

Ben interrupts, "Well you never answer it sir."

In the next scene Ben Stein is sitting in the hallway, expelled, hence the name of the movie. Ben Stein is funny, smart and relentless. You need to be just as relentless and smart in your pursuit of martial arts knowledge. Don't be lazy. Break the *bunkai*, break the application.

Here's a good example: Sports competitors (e.g., judoka) pin people face-up, allowing for a furtherance of the competition because there's leverage the pinned person can use to escape. Cops and security personnel, on the other hand, pin people face-down so that they have little chance of fighting back or getting away. Done properly, it's virtually impossible to escape being held face-down until your captor decides to let you go. Lawrence has known this for years, used the application several times in real life, and taught it to his students.

One day he tried pinning another black belt face-down. This guy was a monster of a man who had played linebacker at a Division One college, and who outweighed him by close to a hundred pounds. Guess what, the hold down didn't work! It shouldn't have come as a surprise, but since Lawrence had never had that much of a mismatch before it was something of a shock when the other guy just stood up. Technique may overcome brute strength in most instances, but certainly not all of them. He'd broken the *bunkai*... and is much wiser for it.

Test it. Ask challenging questions, no matter how awkward. Risk being expelled. You'll be pleasantly surprised by what you might learn.

Making it real...

Accept a little risk when it comes to your training. Be respectful, of course, and be willing to live with the results, but take that risk. Delve deep. Strive to understand why it works, not that it does. And, importantly, discover under what circumstances it doesn't work. Break the *bunkai*.

CHAPTER EIGHTY-THREE

YOGA-IN-A-BOX

"Desire is the key to motivation, but it is determination and commitment to an unrelenting pursuit of your goal, a commitment to excellence, that will enable you to attain the success you seek."

– Mario Andretti

At a local chain bookstore recently put up an end-cap display. The racks of the display were stuffed with New Year's resolution boxes featuring yoga books, yoga mats, special cork bricks, and DVD's covered with beautiful people looking happy, centered and tan. The boxes had wonderful names and they promised, or at least implied, no less than a genetic transformation for purchasing them.

We all know that maybe one percent of the folks who buy these materials are going to actually use them, and those who do will quickly outgrow the Yoga-in-a-

Box and seek a real class with a qualified instructor.

How is Yoga-in-a-Box like the martial arts? The joy and excitement of the beginning of the process is not enough to sustain the practitioner long enough to truly grow in their art, dedication is the key. Not macho teeth-gritting dedication, but calm, focused dedication, deliberately putting one foot in front of the other along the path toward self-betterment.

The euphoria of the new is unsustainable. Satisfaction of hard earned accomplishments, this is much deeper, longer lasting, and more meaningful. It should be sought over euphoria.

Making it real...

We live in a fast food, Yoga-in-a-Box, Cliff Notes, insta-download society, yet we also know that martial artists are different. We want more, and we're willing to work for it. Mostly. Crossing the inevitable plateaus that come with martial arts training is tough, so tough that many folks drop out at that stage. How many times have we seen practitioners earn their *shodan*, their first degree belt, and then quit? On trick that helps keep us going can be a training log. By taking notes in a journal we not only remember what we've learned but also are able to look back and see how far we've come. Oftentimes this can be a source of motivation to persevere when we get bogged down along the road toward mastery.

CHAPTER EIGHTY-FOUR

SEE, DO, TEACH

"In learning you will teach, and in teaching you will learn."

– Phil Collins

As people get around brown belt in their ranking we make an effort to have them teach. The reason is that they need to know how to communicate what they do and to explain the technique, the application, the concept well. Being able to helpfully explain what is being taught is important; it reduces frustration and makes for faster learning.

We have all worked for a boss who has uttered the classic, "Work smarter, not harder" or something equally hackneyed and sloganistic. And then they inevitably walk away leaving us thinking, "Yeah, thanks a lot. That was helpful... not."

But what if the boss dumped the worn out clichés and instead said something along the lines of, "Here, let me show you a trick." Now, *that* is helpful.

Teaching the martial arts is similar, struggling to explain something to others helps you internalize what you've learned and express it in useful ways. How does the "see-do-teach" concept work into this? By brown belt level the basic mechanics of your chosen art should be ingrained. At this level students are expected to be able to see the technique, do the technique, and then teach it.

The deeper understanding that comes with opportunities to educate others is so important to mastery that we believe your martial arts experience cannot be a complete if you don't spend at least a little time teaching or coaching.

Making it real...

Different experiences shine new light on the familiar. To explain a technique you must be able to grasp onto it, to explore it. "See-do-teach" is a clever way to assure that everybody grows. And growth is important; even if the student is one of the few who actually goes on to teach martial arts on a regular basis. If you run a martial arts school, give your senior students opportunities to lead class, or a portion thereof, from time to time. If you're a senior student, on the other hand, ask your instructor to give you a chance to teach. It takes some burden off them while simultaneously helping you grow.

It doesn't have to become a profession, but it will strengthen your understanding and hone your skills in the martial arts.

CHAPTER EIGHTY-FIVE

THE OLD GUYS

"Once the game is over, the king and the pawn go back in the same box."

– Italian Proverb

You know what we like? We like the old guys, the old karateka, the old judoka, the guys with nothing to prove. They smile easily, and are just all around pleasant to converse with. What we don't like... well, here's a story to illustrate that point:

I was at a tournament. The guy running the show was in his eighties, looked sixty, and smiled readily. He made decisions easily, no drama if something happened that was out of the ordinary, he just fixed it. He didn't deal with it; he fixed it, a big difference in my book.

Then of course there was the other guy that glowered sternly at everybody with his best "*sensei* eyes," you know, like a Japanese woodcut from the age of the samurai. This guy would do the eyebrow lift thing, then turn his attention to the object of his critical view. It is as if he had taken a mail order course called, "How to look Like a *Sensei* in Eleven Easy Lessons." And frankly he had not done well, but did learn the essential bad acting, "Lift of the eyebrow," in Lesson One.

At the end of the day, the old guy went around and shook hands, thanked people for their participation, smiled a lot, smiled some more, and said, "Hope to see you next time."

The other guy, on the other hand, he cornered me. I'm sure I was just the guy in proximity, and what followed could have happened to anyone. He reached into the back pocket of his *gi* (seriously; how many *gi*s actually come with pockets, he must have sewn that in) and pulled a photo out of his wallet.

"You know who that is?"

"Uh, that's you on the right," I guessed. The picture was older and had been tattered by years of lying in his wallet.

"Yeah but, next to me, who's that?"

I looked for a moment at the bent picture, "I, gotta say, I don't know." He stabbed his finger toward the picture again. "That's Joe Lewis. Me and Joe Lewis!" For those who may not remember, Joe Lewis dominated the karate fighting circuit in the 1970's.

I could see the pride on his face, but to it was a very awkward moment. This guy and I, we had seen each other around, but never really spoken and he had just bushwhacked me on the way out the door to show me his picture of him and Joe Lewis.

Two guys at the tournament: One guy with nothing to prove, and the other guy who despite all his apparent accomplishments still needed to add more to who he was.

Yeah, we like the old guys. Easy, smiling, nothing to prove...

With age comes a sense of place.

Making it real...

The four key elements of how you are perceived by others include appearance, attire, demeanor, and behavior. It is important to know how we come across, particularly as impacted by our demeanor and behavior, since oftentimes we are perceived differently than we think we are. There's a common business tool, the 360° review, that's designed for just that purpose. It asks a structured set of questions of those around you, employer, peers, and employees, who can judge your performance. Modified for use in the *dojo*, create a short questionnaire for students and fellow instructors to fill out a couple times a year. The exact questions you ask are somewhat less important than the feedback you receive, be sure they are open-ended enough to obtain candid responses. In this fashion you'll know if you're coming across like the needy, insecure guy at the tournament or like the wise older guy who ran it. Take the feedback seriously and it will help you grow.

CHAPTER EIGHTY-SIX

SMITH'S RULES OF DESIGN, #4

"I have yet to see any problem, however complicated, which, when you looked at it in the right way, did not become still more complicated."

– Poul Anderson

In the August 2008 issue of *Popular Mechanics* magazine is a great article titled, "Smith's Rules of Design." In this chapter we'll discuss Rule #4: "Create 'transparent' technologies, ones that are easily understood by the users, and promote local innovation."

As martial artists, how often do we complicate what we teach? Importantly, how often do we do so unintentionally? When teaching applications, forms, or whatever to beginners we tend to break things down into component parts, build the skills, and then recombine them into a larger whole. Sounds good, but an unintended consequence is that oftentimes students miss the overarching goal.

Take, for example, the classic "corkscrewing" karate punch: One fluid movement allows impact at multiple ranges—short uppercut, mid-range standing fist, longer range fore-fist—but folks oftentimes only look to the final point of impact at range, hence miss two of the three techniques represented by that movement. Another common misconception is ubiquitous use of the term "block" when we are really trying to describe the way one should receive an attack.

Transparency is virtually always missing in how we teach *kata* too. While instructors might show an application or two, invariably the conversation delves to techniques, tactics rather than principles, so the larger story is missed. This can lead to a whole host of misunderstandings, the least of which is that *kata* has no martial value since the most commonly shown *bunkai* are meaningless.

Making it real...

Clearly there's value in breaking complex things down into component parts, there's so much to learn in the martial arts that it's simply indigestible otherwise, but be cautious and cognizant in doing that such that the larger picture is not lost. This is most easily accomplished via a lesson plan. While it's easier to "wing it," building an outline with whatever level of detail you find most useful of what you need students to know and how you'll lead them there makes for a richer, more meaningful experience. In this fashion you can build needed transparency into your instruction—lessons can build upon each other in a logical format, with knowledge checks at key milestones along the way, so that interconnections won't be lost. Ultimately strategies and tactics align, and folks truly understand what you're teaching in a practical and functional way.

CHAPTER EIGHTY-SEVEN

CHICKEN WIRE, BLACK PAINT AND NEON, OH, MY!

"I thoroughly disapprove of duels. If a man should challenge me, I would take him kindly and forgivingly by the hand, lead him to a quiet place, and kill him.

– Mark Twain

Recently we took part in a seminar with Rory Miller, the author of *Meditations on Violence, Conflict Communication*, and many other outstanding books. Instead of the usual training hall-type environment, the seminar was held at a nightclub in downtown Seattle called *Motor*, owned by one of our students, Travis.

What an environment: Chicken wire, tables, chairs, black paint, and neon, a bit of a shock for folks used to practicing in the clean, controlled, clutter-free environments found in most *dojo*!

Rory likes to say that "fights happen in places," a far more profound statement that it seems at face value. He takes people places they have never been before when it comes to scenarios, not because they don't want to go, but because of the realism and forethought inherent in what he presents. His focus on the potential aftermath of the decisions made throughout the exercises is always insightful; it brings out stuff that's never occurred to most attendees. We mentioned the "baby" drill earlier; it's but one of many examples.

Without going into specifics, Rory took the group through one scenario that involved a shooting. In two short sentences he took a person to a point where he broke one of the primary tenets of his professional training... and put his life at risk had that scenario been a real event. The scenario wasn't about right or wrong, it was about knowing our own internal rules and how that affects our decision-making.

Beyond the drills, the club itself made a huge difference when it came to the hands-on aspects of the seminar. People going rolling underneath the bar, others going stand-up in the middle of the dance floor, and one guy choking another with the rope normally used for crowd control, it was far from anything we've ever experienced in any *dojo*. Don't get us wrong, it wasn't a free-for-all. Activities were safe, well-managed, realistic, educational, and a heck a lot of fun.

Truly eye opening, such training is a real channel changer.

Making it real...

Fights happen in places, and those places are rarely if ever the pristine hardwood floor of a traditional *dojo* where everyone is wearing a *dogi*. Change things up from time to time, practicing in your street clothes outdoors, in the rain, at a nightclub, in a stairwell, in a swimming pool, anywhere that forces you to compensate for the bad footing, impromptu weapons, or other environmental hazards. Such training obviously needs to be carefully controlled to assure participant safety, but done right it's an unbelievably valuable experience for participants.

CONCLUSION

"In the attitude of silence the soul finds the path in a clearer light, and what is elusive and deceptive resolves itself into crystal clearness."

– Mahatma Gandhi

In this book we presented you with an 87-fold path designed to broaden your perspective of the martial arts. For those concepts that resonated we hope that you have taken actions toward implementation and that you are already seeing positive changes in your outlook and your training. Where we have led, you've followed, but now it's your turn to forge the way. As Ralph Waldo Emerson (1803 – 1882) once wrote, "Do not go where the path may lead, go instead where there is no path and leave a trail." Wherever you go from, enjoy the journey.

Yours in *budo*,

Kris and Lawrence

Kris Wilder

Kris Wilder is the head instructor and owner of West Seattle Karate Academy. He started practicing the martial arts at the age of fifteen. Over the years he has earned black belt rankings in three styles, *Goju-Ryu* karate (5th *dan*), taekwondo (2nd *dan*), and judo (1st *dan*), in which he has competed in senior nationals and international tournaments. He is the author of eight books including two *USA Book News* Best Books Award finalists and a *ForeWord Magazine* Book of the Year Award finalist. He also stars in two instructional DVDs.

Kris has been blessed with the opportunity to train under skilled instructors, including Olympic athletes, state champions, national champions, and gifted martial artists who take their lineage directly from the founders of their systems. He teaches seminars worldwide, focusing on growing a person's martial technique and their understanding, whatever their art may be. Kris also serves as a National Representative for the University of New Mexico's Institute of Traditional Martial Arts.

Kris spent about 15 years in the political and public affairs area, working for campaigns from the local to national level. During this consulting career he was periodically on staff for elected officials. His work also involved lobbying and corporate affairs. He is currently a member of The Order of St. Francis (OSF); the OSF is one of many active Apostolic Christian Orders.

Kris lives in Seattle, Washington with his son Jackson. You can contact him directly at wskadojo@gmail.com.

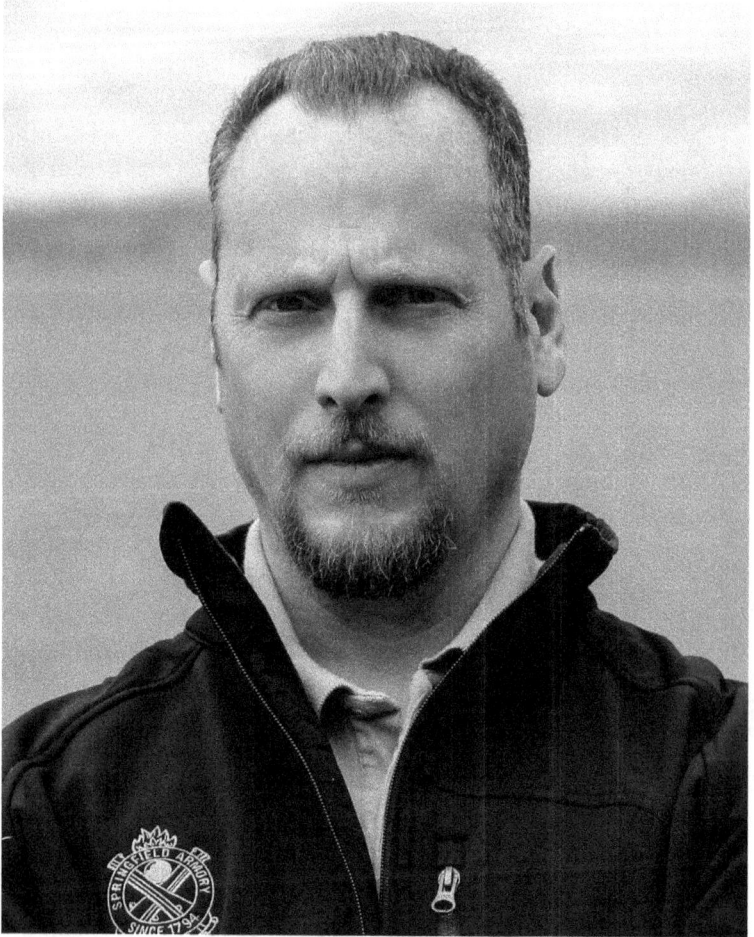

Lawrence A. Kane

Since 1970, Lawrence has studied and taught traditional Asian martial arts, medieval European combat, and modern close-quarter weapon techniques. Working stadium security part-time over 26 years he was involved in hundreds of violent altercations, but got paid to watch football. A world-renown judicious use-of-force expert, he was once interviewed in English by a reporter from a Swiss magazine for an article that was published in French, and finds that oddly amusing.

To pay the bills he develops IT strategies for an aerospace company where he gets to play with billions of dollars of other people's money and make really important decisions. He has saved the company more than $2.1B by multi-sourcing select IT infrastructure elements to internal and external suppliers and benchmarking resultant contracts.

He is also the best-selling author of eleven books, including two *ForeWord Magazine* Book of the Year Award finalists, an *eLit Book Awards* Bronze prize, a *Next Generation Indie Book Awards* finalist, and three *USA Book News* Best Books Award finalists. A founding technical consultant to University of New Mexico's Institute of Traditional Martial Arts, he also has written numerous articles on martial arts, self-defense, countervailing force, and related topics.

Lawrence lives in Seattle, Washington with his son Joey and wife Julie. You can contact him directly at lakane@ix.netcom.com.

OTHER WORKS
BY THE AUTHORS

Non-Fiction Books

1) Dirty Ground (Kane/Wilder)

"Fills a void in martial arts training." – Loren W. Christensen, Martial Arts Masters Hall of Fame member

This book addresses a significant gap in most martial arts training, the tricky space that lies between sport and combat applications when you need to control a person without injuring him (or her). Techniques in this region are called "drunkle," named after the drunken uncle disrupting a family gathering. Understanding how to deal with combat, sport, and drunkle situations is vital because appropriate use of force is codified in law and actions that do not accommodate these regulations can have severe repercussions. Martial arts techniques must be adapted to best fit the situation you find yourself in. This book shows you how.

2) How to Win a Fight (Kane/Wilder)

"It is the ultimate course in self-defense and will help you survive and get through just about any violent situation or attack." – Jeff Rivera, bestselling author

More than three million Americans are involved in a violent physical encounter every year. Develop the fortitude to walk away when you can and prevail when you must. Defense begins by scanning your environment, recognizing hazards and escape routes, and using verbal de-escalation to defuse tense situations. If a fight is unavoidable, the authors offer clear guidance for being the victor, along with advice on legal implications, including how to handle a police interview after the attack.

3) Lessons from the Dojo Floor (Wilder)

"Helps each reader, from white belt to black belt, look at and understand why he or she trains." – Michael E. Odell, Isshin-Ryu Northwest Okinawa Karate Association

In the vein of Dave Lowry, a thought provoking collection of short vignettes that entertains while it educates. Packed with straightforward, easy, and quick to read sections that range from profound to insightful to just plain amusing, anyone with an affinity for martial arts can benefit from this material.

4) Martial Arts Instruction (Kane)

"Boeing trains hundreds of security officers, Kane's ideas will help us be more effective." – Gregory A. Gwash, Chief Security Officer, Boeing

While the old adage, "those who can't do, teach," is not entirely true, all too often "those who can do" cannot teach effectively. This book is unique in that it offers a holistic approach to teaching martial arts; incorporating elements of educational theory and communication techniques typically overlooked in *budo* (warrior arts). Teachers will improve their abilities to motivate, educate, and retain students, while students interested in the martial arts will develop a better understanding of what instructional method best suits their needs.

5) <u>Sensei Mentor Teacher Coach</u> (Wilder/Kane)

"Finally a book that will actually move the needle in closing the leadership skills gap found in all aspects of our society." – Dan Roberts, CEO and President, Ouellette & Associates

Many books weave platitudes, promising the keys to success in leadership, secrets that will transform you into the great leader, the one. The fact of the matter is, however, that true leadership really isn't about you. It's about giving back, offering your best to others so that they can find the best in themselves. The methodologies in this book help you become the leader you were meant to be by bringing your goals and other peoples' needs together to create a powerful, combined vision. Learn how to access the deeper aspects of who you are, your unique qualities, and push them forward in actionable ways. Acquire this vital information and advance your leadership journey today.

6) <u>Scaling Force</u> (Kane/Miller)

"If you're serious about learning how the application of physical force works—before, during and after the fact—I cannot recommend this book highly enough." – Lieutenant Jon Lupo, New York State Police

Conflict and violence cover a broad range of behaviors, from intimidation to murder, and require an equally broad range of responses. A kind word will not resolve all situations, nor will wristlocks, punches, or even a gun. This book introduces the full range of options, from skillfully doing nothing to employing deadly force. You will understand the limits of each type of force, when specific levels may be appropriate, the circumstances under which you may have to apply them, and the potential costs, legally and personally, of your decision.

7) <u>Surviving Armed Assaults</u> (Kane)

"This book will be an invaluable resource for anyone walking the warrior's path, and anyone who is interested in this vital topic." – Lt. Col. Dave Grossman, Director, Warrior Science Group

A sad fact is that weapon-wielding thugs victimize 1,773,000 citizens every year in the United States alone. Even martial artists are not immune from this deadly threat. Consequently, self-defense training that does not consider the very real possibility of an armed attack is dangerously incomplete. Whether you live in the city or countryside, you should be both mentally and physically prepared to deal with an unprovoked armed assault at any time. Preparation must be comprehensive enough to account for the plethora of pointy objects, blunt instruments, explosive devices, and deadly projectiles that someday could be used against you. This extensive book teaches proven survival skills that can keep you safe.

8) <u>The Little Black Book of Violence</u> (Kane/Wilder)

"This book will save lives!" – Alain Burrese, JD, former US Army 2nd Infantry Division Scout Sniper School instructor

Men commit 80 % of all violent crimes and are twice
as likely to become the victims of aggressive behavior.
This book is primarily written for men ages 15 to 35,
and contains more than mere self-defense techniques.
You will learn crucial information about street
survival that most martial arts instructors don't even
know. Discover how to use awareness, avoidance,
and de-escalation to help stave off violence, know
when it's prudent to fight, and understand how to do
so effectively.

9) The Way of Kata (Kane/Wilder)

*"This superb book is essential reading for all
those who wish to understand the highly effective
techniques, concepts, and strategies that the kata
were created to record."* – Iain Abernethy, British
Combat Association Hall of Fame member

The ancient masters developed *kata*, or "formal
exercises," as fault-tolerant methods to preserve
their unique, combat-proven fighting systems.
Unfortunately, they also deployed a two-track system
of instruction where an outer circle of students
unknowingly received modified forms with critical
details or important principles omitted. Only the
select inner circle that had gained a master's trust
and respect would be taught *okuden waza*, the
powerful hidden applications of *kata*. The theory
of deciphering *kata* applications (*kaisai no genri*)
was once a great mystery revealed only to trusted
disciples of the ancient masters in order to protect
the secrets of their systems. Even today, while the
basic movements of *kata* are widely known, advanced
practical applications and sophisticated techniques

frequently remain hidden from the casual observer. The principles and rules for understanding *kata* are largely unknown. This groundbreaking book unveils these methods, not only teaching you how to analyze your *kata* to understand what it is trying to tell you, but also helping you to utilize your fighting techniques more effectively.

10) The Way of Martial Arts for Kids (Wilder)

"Written in a personable, engaging style that will appeal to kids and adults alike." – Laura Vanderpool, martial artist

Based on centuries of traditions, martial arts training can be a positive experience for kids. The book helps you and yours get the most out of class. It shows how just about any child can become one of those few exemplary learners who excel in the training hall as well as in life. Written to children, it is also for parents too. After all, while the martial arts instructor knows his art, no one knows his/her child better than the parent. Together you can help your child achieve just about anything... The advice provided is straightforward, easy to understand, and written with a child-reader in mind so that it can either be studied by the child and/or read together with the parent.

11) The Way of Sanchin Kata (Wilder)

"This book has been sorely needed for generations!" – Philip Starr, National Chairman, Yiliquan Martial Arts Association

When Karate or *Ti* was first developed in Okinawa it was about using technique and extraordinary power to end a fight instantly. These old ways of generating remarkable power are still accessible, but they are purposefully hidden in *Sanchin kata* for the truly dedicated to find. This book takes the practitioner to new depths of practice by breaking down the form piece-by-piece, body part by body part, so that the very foundation of the *kata* is revealed. Every chapter, concept, and application is accompanied by a "Test It" section, designed for you to explore and verify the *kata* for yourself. *Sanchin kata* really comes alive when you feel the thrill of having those hidden teachings speak to you across the ages through your body. Simply put, once you read this book and test what you have learned, your karate will never be the same.

12) The Way to Black Belt (Kane/Wilder)

"It is so good I wish I had written it myself." – Hanshi Patrick McCarthy, Director, International Ryukyu Karate Research Society

Cut to the very core of what it means to be successful in the martial arts. Earning a black belt can be the most rewarding experience of a lifetime, but getting there takes considerable planning. Whether your interests are in the classical styles of Asia or in today's Mixed Martial Arts, this book prepares you to meet every challenge. Whatever your age, whatever your gender, you will benefit from the wisdom of master martial artists around the globe, including Iain Abernethy, Dan Anderson, Loren Christensen, Jeff Cooper, Wim Demeere, Aaron Fields, Rory Miller,

Martina Sprague, Phillip Starr, and many more, who share more than 300 years of combined training experience. Benefit from their guidance during your development into a first-class black belt.

Fiction Books:

1) <u>Blinded by the Night</u> **(Kane)**

"Kane's expertise in matters of mayhem shines throughout." – Steve Perry, bestselling author

Richard Hayes is a Seattle cop. After 25 years with the PD he thinks he knows everything there is to know about predators. The dregs of society like rapists, murderers, gang bangers, and child molesters are just another day at the office. Commonplace criminals become the least of his problems when he goes hunting for a serial killer and runs into a real monster. The creature not only attacks him, but merely gets pissed off when he shoots it. In the head. Twice! Surviving that fight is only the beginning. Richard discovers that the vampire he destroyed was the ruler of an eldritch realm he never dreamed existed. By some archaic rule, having defeated the monster's sovereign in battle, Richard becomes their new king. Now he is responsible for a host of horrors who stalk the night, howl at the moon, and shamble through the darkness. But, why would these creatures willingly obey a human? When it comes to human predators, Richard is a seasoned veteran, yet with paranormal ones he is but a rookie. He must navigate a web of intrigue and survive long enough to discover how a regular guy can tangle with supernatural creatures and prevail. One mistake and things surely won't end well...

DVDs:

1) <u>121 Killer Appz</u> (Wilder/Kane)

"Quick and brutal, the way karate is meant to be." – Eric Parsons, Founder, Karate for Life Foundation

You know the *kata*, now it is time for the applications. *Gekisai (Dai Ni), Saifa, Seiyunchin, Seipai, Kururunfa, Suparinpei, Sanseiru, Shisochin,* and *Seisan kata* are covered. If you ever wondered what purpose a move from a *Goju Ryu* karate form was for, wonder no longer. This DVD contains no discussion, just a no-nonsense approach to one application after another. It is sure to provide deeper understanding to your *kata* practice and stimulate thought on determining your own applications to the *Goju Ryu* karate forms.

2) <u>Sanchin Kata: Three Battles Karate Kata</u> (Wilder)

"A cornucopia of martial arts knowledge." – Shawn Kovacich, endurance high-kicking world record holder (as certified by the Guinness Book of World Records)

A traditional training method for building karate power *Sanchin kata*, or Three Battles Sequence, is an ancient form that can be traced back to the roots of karate. Some consider it the missing link between

Chinese kung fu and Okinawan karate. *Sanchin kata* is known to develop extraordinary quickness and generate remarkable power. This program breaks down the form piece by piece, body part by body part, so that the hidden details of the *kata* are revealed. Regular practice of *Sanchin kata* conditions the body, trains correct alignment, and teaches the essential structure needed for generating power within all of your karate movements. Many karate practitioners believe that *Sanchin kata* holds the key to mastering the traditional martial arts. Though it can be one of the simplest forms to learn, it is simultaneously one of the most difficult to perfect. This DVD complements the book The Way of Sanchin Kata, providing in-depth exploration of the form, with detailed instruction of the essential posture, linking the spine, generating power, and demonstration of the complete *kata*.

www.ingramcontent.com/pod-product-compliance
Lightning Source LLC
Chambersburg PA
CBHW071314090426
42738CB00012B/2694